Longman Exam Practice Kits

A-level
German

Alex Reich
Alasdair McKeane

LONGMAN

Series Editors
Geoff Black and Stuart Wall

Titles available

GCSE	A-level
Biology	Biology
Business Studies	British and European Modern History
Chemistry	Business Studies
English	Chemistry
French	Economics
Geography	French
German	Geography
Higher Mathematics	German
Information Systems	Mathematics
Mathematics	Physics
Physics	Psychology
Science	Sociology

Addison Wesley Longman Ltd,
Edinburgh Gate, Harlow,
Essex CM20 2JE, England
and Associated Companies throughout the World

First Published 1998

ISBN 0582-31247-7

British Library Cataloguing-in-Publication Data
A catalogue record for this book is available from the British Library.

Set by 34 in 11/13pt Baskerville
Produced by Longman Singapore Publishers Pte
Printed in Singapore

Contents

Acknowledgements

The following examination boards have kindly granted permission to reproduce material from their specimen syllabuses.

Edexcel Foundation (London Examinations) (acknowledged in the text as London)
The Associated Examining Board (acknowledged in the text as AEB Specimen Question)
Northern Ireland Council for the Curriculum Examinations and Assessment (acknowledged in the text as CCEA)
University of Cambridge Local Examinations Syndicate (acknowledged in the text as UCLES)

Edexcel Foundation, London Examinations accepts no responsibility whatsoever for the accuracy or method of working in the answers given.

Any answers or hints on answers are the sole responsibility of the authors and have not been provided or approved by the Associated Examining Board.

We are also grateful to the following for permission to reproduce copyright material:

Audi for permission to reproduce an advertisement of the Audi A4 (see page 89). SpiegelVerlag for permission to reproduce an article from *Der Spiegel*, March 1996 (see page 97) and for permission to redraw the charts from *Der Spiegel*, April 1996 (see page 45). Verband Deutscher Verkehrsunternehmen (VDV) for permission to reproduce an advertisement of German Association VDV and German National Railways DB AG (see page 97). Wilhelm Heyne Verlag GMBH & Co.KG for permission to reproduce an advertisement of their publications (see page 96).

Whilst every effort has been made to trace the owners of copyright material we take this opportunity to offer our apologies to any copyright holders whose rights we may have unwittingly infringed. In particular we would welcome any information about the copyright owners for the advert 'Ich rauche' on page 64 and the advert 'Typisch Airtours' on page 88 whom we have been unable to trace.

Study skills

Introduction

This chapter gives many hints on how to study effectively. The first section will apply to virtually any A-level or AS-level subject, while the second looks at each of the study skills which are especially relevant to learning German. You will find advice on using dictionaries, learning vocabulary, speaking, listening, writing and reading.

Sixth Form study skills

Efficient studying is vital if you are to achieve success. The following hints will help you to make the best use of your A-level or AS-level course. In the main, these hints apply to whatever subject you are studying. Help with skills which apply mainly to German is given later in this chapter (see pages 4–14). The key to success is being in control of the learning process, being actively involved in it and taking responsibility for your share of the learning package. It really is pretty feeble to say 'My teacher's job is to motivate me.' You should look for ways to motivate yourself by learning efficiently and therefore effectively.

Materials

Make sure you have the equipment you need for lessons and for study. You should always turn up for lessons with a pen, a coloured pen or a pencil to provide a contrast, and paper, as well as the books, work and notes required for the session and a dictionary.

Having the right equipment is such an obvious point that it is too often overlooked.

Assignments

You will have many more assignments to complete than when you were doing your GCSE German course. There will probably be texts to prepare, regular language work to be done, notes to be written up, vocabulary to be learnt, presentations to prepare and listening exercises to be done.

An A-level in a modern language differs from other subjects in that students obtain the greatest value from work which is short-term. So preparing a text is of most value before the lesson in which that text is discussed. Equally, this week's language assignment is most valuable to you this week. So the important message about assignments is: **Do it NOW!** If you can keep on top of your work, you save the time you might spend deciding when and in what order to do things, as well as gaining maximum advantage from the work you do.

Your work diary

A well-kept work diary helps enormously in keeping up to date. You should record what has been set, by whom, for when, and the date you completed it.

If you take an active part in knowing what topic is being studied, when the work on it is due in and what aims the teacher has in mind, the value of the whole process is enhanced. You will also be spared those awful moments of unforeseen crisis when too many deadlines coincide.

Places for study

You will need to have a regular place for study, preferably one which is undisturbed. It should have good lighting, a steady table or desk to write at, your notes to hand and a dictionary.

If you can aim to have a regular seat in the library or study area at school or college, that is probably psychologically beneficial, too.

Distractions

Many students attempt to study while actually doing something else, such as listening to music, chatting to friends, watching TV or snacking. **Don't kid yourself that you are studying when you are not**. Instead, use some of these activities mentioned as a reward so that you have something to look forward to when you have ended a work session.

Times

Regular study is an important aim. Experience suggests that, with very few exceptions, students who attend more than 95 per cent of lessons always achieve an A-level grade no matter how weak they are, whereas those whose appearance in class is less frequent do not always pass. As a rough guide, you should aim to study between 35 and 45 hours per week, including timetabled lessons. Many adults work about that number of hours weekly. This will mean that you should be spending about twelve to fifteen hours a week on your A-level German, or six to eight hours on AS-level German, which includes making sensible use of private study time.

It is generally reckoned that a regular pattern of work is more productive than a random one. So if you have regular times in the week when you do your studying for each subject, you are more likely to do an even amount of work across your subjects, and are also more likely to do those extra activities which make the difference between average and excellent students.

A final point on timing is that you should not work for too long without a break. Psychologists reckon that sessions of about 45 minutes are the longest that most people can concentrate for without a short break.

Notes and files

Efficient organisation of teaching and learning materials is a key to success at A-level. It is unlikely that teachers will just use one textbook as a source, and you will probably receive a good quantity of photocopied material during your two-year course. To be able to revise effectively, it is essential to keep this material in good order using an A4 lever-arch file, some section separators and a hole punch.

Your teacher(s) should make clear to you which topics you are studying. Aim to collect a complete set of all materials given out, all work done and all notes you make in class on the topic, and to file it separately.

It is advisable not to carry too large a quantity of notes around with you, in case of loss. The sensible approach is to have the work in progress with you and a bank of older material at home.

As well as collecting notes given to you, you should make sure that you always listen or read with a pen in your hand. Reading without notes is reading lost. The act of writing a note of vocabulary you did not know in a passage tends to fix it in your mind and, if your filing system is good, you will have the vocabulary notes next to the text when you come to review it. Remember that nothing that your teacher says is copyright – so write it down.

There is benefit to be gained from writing up a neat copy of a translation into German or an essay in German after the teacher has corrected your first version. It is likely to prove useful when revising, as well as drawing your attention to shortcomings in your first version.

Information technology

Increasingly, students are arriving in the Sixth Form with information technology skills which they wish to use in their Sixth Form studies. If your keyboard skills are good, you may well find it useful to write some of your work on a word-processor, assuming your teacher is happy to accept it. However, there are a few pitfalls connected with the learning of a foreign language. First, you will not be able to use a word-processor in the A-level examination unless you have a special dispensation because of some handicap you suffer. Second, it may not be very useful for note-taking unless you really are very fluent in its use and you have a relatively portable machine. Third, you will need to decide what to do about the umlaut and the *Eszett or scharfes s (β)*. Both of these are vital to German at A-level. Ideally you need a program which produces these characters. The most popular word-processors can insert these. Make sure you know how.

Spell checkers and electronic dictionaries are available in German for use with popular programs. At the time of writing (early 1997), no examination board will allow you to consult an electronic dictionary in an examination. And spell checkers in German

▶ presuppose that you will recognise the right answer when you are offered it
▶ mean that you still have to know how the adjective endings work in each circumstance.

Spreadsheets, not normally thought of as a word-processing tool, can often be adapted for keeping a personal vocabulary list up to date.

Finally, beware of spending too much time prettifying your work via the DTP wonders of your program. Word-processing is merely a tool, and if it takes up more of your time than using a pen, then use a pen!

Absence

At some point in the two years it is likely that you will be unfortunate enough to be unwell, or you may be away visiting universities or colleges. It is important to realise that **you** need to take steps to make up what you have missed. The course does not stop merely because you don't happen to be present!

On your return, you should

▶ ask your teacher for materials used and a note of the work covered
▶ borrow and copy (or photocopy) notes from a reliable fellow-student
▶ negotiate with your teacher about which assignments need to be done and when
▶ actually work through the material you have collected.

Study skills for learners of foreign languages

Dictionary work

Many students will be well used to using a simple German–English dictionary from their GCSE course. You may already own one which you know your way round. But if you don't already own a dictionary, you should aim to have one before you go very far in your A-level course. It is important to have one which is big enough to contain the majority of words you need, but which is not so big that you are discouraged from bringing it to lessons. Aim to pay between £7 and £25 for a German–English dictionary.

Before making the purchase, check with your teacher whether your examination board allows you to take dictionaries into the examination, and if so, whether they allow English–German or insist on German–German. Your teacher may recommend a particular dictionary, or would prefer you to have one type rather than the other. If you are not given any specific advice, go for a dictionary which shows the plurals of German nouns and which has been out for a relatively short length of time, say less than ten years since its last revision.

German–English dictionaries

The main part of the dictionary is taken up with two alphabetical lists of words. It is important to take the time to get to know the other information in the entries and to learn how to use the information given.

In particular, you need to be familiar with the majority of abbreviations commonly used in the text. Make sure you know where to check the abbreviations in your dictionary, and how to use the verb table to produce verbs which work.

Looking up a German word

When you look up a German word, you may find a number of possible English translations, listed with the most common first. You will then have to use your common sense to work out which meaning is most likely in the context.

You may find that a word is not listed. This may mean that it is a past participle. Check if it begins with *ge-*, or one of the inseparable prefixes such as *be-*, *emp-*, *ent-*, or *ver-*, or if it ends in *-en*. Then use either the rules for formation of regular verbs to deduce the infinitive, or consult a table of strong (irregular) verbs. Alternatively, it may be an irregular imperfect form. Again, consult the strong verb table. The grammar chapter also tells you how to use a verb table (see page 28).

Below is a page from a modern dictionary with the features highlighted.

phonetic script — **tuberkulös** [-ku'lø:s] *adj.* tuberculous, tubercular; ~ **ose** [-ku'lø:zə] *f* (-; -n) tuberculosis; ~ **osenverdächtig** *adj.* suspected of tuberculosis.

optional e in Genitive singular — **Tuch** [tu:x] *n* (-[e]s; -e) cloth; fabric; (-[e]s, -er) shawl; scarf, neckerchief, duster; rag; *das wirkt auf ihn wie ein rotes* ~ that's a red rag to him; ~ **ballen** *m* bale of cloth; ~**fabrik** *f* cloth factory; ~**handel**

neuter noun — *m* cloth trade, drapery; ~ **handler** *m* (wool(l)en) draper; ~ **handlung** *f*, ~ **laden** *m* draper's shop; ~ **macher** *m* cloth-maker.

adjective — **tüchtig** ['tyçtiç] **I.** *adj.* able, fit; (cap)able, competent, qualified; efficient; clever, skil(l)ful; proficient, experienced; excellent; good, considerable; powerful, strong; thorough; ~ *in* (*dat.*) good

adverb — at, proficient (*or* well versed) in; ~*er Esser* hearty eater; **II.** *adv.* vigorously, with a vengeance, like mad, thoroughly, well; *coilog really* ~*arbeiten* work hard; ~ *essen* eat heartily; ~ *verprügeln* give a sound thrashing; ~ **keit** *f* (-) ability, efficiency; cleverness; proficiency; excellence *sportliche* ~ sporting prowess.

Tuch...: ~ **waren** *f/pl.* cloths, drapery *sg.*; ~ **zeichen** *aer.* *n* ground panel.

Tücke ['tykə] *f* (-; -n) malice, spite; perfidy, insidiousness; trick (*of fate, memory*); **oisch** *adj.*

plural — malicious, spiteful; insidious (*a. disease* = malignant); vicious (*a. animal, blow*); treacherous (*a. ice, road, etc.*).

feminine noun — **Tugend** ['tu:gənt] *f* (-; -en) virtue; *es sich zur* ~ *machen, zu inf.* make a virtue of *doing a th.*, → *Not*; **haft** *adj.* virtuous; **reich** *adj.* most virtuous; **sam** *adj.* virtuous; chaste.

genitive singular — **Tüll** [tyl] *m* (-s; -e) tulle; ~**e** ['tylə] *f* (-; -n) socket; spout; ~ **spitzen** *f/pl.* net lace.

Tulpe ['tulpə] *f* (-; -n) *bot.* tulip; ~ **nzwiebel** *f* tulipbulb.

Tumor ['tu:mɔr] *med.* *m* (-s; -moren) tumour.

Tumult [tu'mult] *m* (-;[e]s; -e) tumult; riot, uproar; row.

medical / *masculine noun* — **tun** [tu:n] *v/t.* (*irr., h.*) do; perform, make; → *machen*; put (*to school, into the bag, etc.*); make (*remark, request*); take (*jump, oath*); nichts ~ do nothing; so ~, *als ob* make *or* act as if, pretend to

range of translation contexts — *inf.*; würdig, *etc.*, ~ assume an air of dignity, etc.; ~ *Sie ganz, als ob Sie zu Hause wären* make yourself quite at home!; *was hat er dir getan?* what has he done to you?; *damit ist es nicht getan* that's not enough; *es tut nichts* it doesn't matter, never mind; *es tut sich (et)was* something is going on (*or* is in the wind *or* is brewing); *es tut nichts zur Sache* it is of no significance, that is neither here nor there; *das tut man nicht!* that is not done!; *tu doch nicht so!* don't make a fuss!, *was ist zu* ~? what is to be done?

Looking up an English word

Looking up an English word to find the German equivalent is more tricky. To be sure of having chosen the right word, follow some or all of the following steps:

(a) Make sure you know if you want a noun, adjective, verb, etc.
(b) After finding the German word, check it by looking it up in the German–English section. You should get the word you started with, or one which means the same thing in the same context.

(c) Beware of choosing *Fremdwörter* from a list in preference to a German-root word. They may seem the same as the English word but often the *Fremdwörter* have a more specialised meaning and usage than their English equivalent.

(d) If the English verb is followed by a preposition, make sure you have found the exact equivalent usage in German, and that you know which case follows the German preposition.

Below is a page from a modern dictionary, with the features highlighted.

phonetic script **di-vulge** [daɪˈvʌldʒ] *vt. Geheimnis etc.* enthüllen. preisgeben

dix-ie[1] [ˈdɪksɪ] *s. sl.* **1.** Kochgeschirr *n;* **2.** , 'Gulaschka,none' *f.*

transitive verb Dix-ie [ˈdɪksɪ] → *Dixieland;*

D-mark [ˈdiːmaːk] *s.* Deutsche Mark, (f)

slang **do** [duː;dʊ] **I** *v/t. [irr.]* **1.** tun, machen: *what can I ~ for you?* womit kann ich dienen?; *what does he ~ for a living?* womit verdient er sein Brot?; ~ *right* recht tun; → *done* 1; **2.** tan, ausführen, sich

gender of noun beschäftigen mit. verrichten. vollbringen. erledigen. *business* Geschäfte machen; ~ *one's duty* s–e Pflicht tun; ~ *German* Deutsch lernen; ~ *Shakespeare* Shakespeare durchnehmen *od.* behandeln;

noun (substantive) *my work is done* m–e Arbeit ist getan *od.* fertig; ~ *60 miles per hour* 60 Meilen die Stunde fahren; *It can't be done* es geht nicht; ~ *one's best* sein Bestes tun, sich alle Mühe geben; ~ *better* **a)** (et.)

different meanings Besseres tun *od.* leisten, **b)** sich verbessern; → *done;* **3.** herstellen, anfertigen: ~ *a translation* e–e Übersetzung machen; ~ *a portrait* ein Porträt malen; **4.** *j-m et.* tun, zufügen, erweisen, gewähren: ~

examples of idioms *s.o. harm* j-m schaden; ~ *s.o. an injustice* j-m ein Unrecht zufügen, j-m unrecht tun; *these pills ~ me (no) good* diese Pillen elfen mir (nicht); **5.** bewirken, erreichen: *I did it* ich habe es geschafft;

Vocabulary learning

To be successful at A-level you will need to know a wide range of vocabulary. Your knowledge will be of three kinds:

1 **Active**   you can readily use words accurately in context.
2 **Passive**   you would not necessarily use a word yourself, but you know what it means.
3 **Deductive**   you do not know the meaning of the word for sure, but can work out pretty well what it means from the context, from the form of the word and from the root words, prefixes and suffixes it contains.

You need to have a regular method of noting, classifying and learning new vocabulary as you come across it. Updating a personal vocabulary notebook or file is a good activity for private study sessions.

Probably the most useful way of keeping notes is by topic. They can then be filed with the topic and used in conjunction with the teaching material for revision. The *Longman A-level Study Guide German* contains a thorough topic-based list.

Similarly, there is something to be said for noting whether verbs are weak (regular) or strong (irregular) and, if strong, what the imperfect and perfect tense are, and also whether the verb takes *sein* as its auxiliary in the perfect and other compound tenses.

Noting vocabulary is a first step to knowing it. But you might also need to set aside time for short bursts of active learning. As well as noting vocabulary as a matter of habit, you could try some of the following ways to actively learn it:

► writing new material out five or ten times on scrap paper
► writing yourself tests to be done a day or two later
► making a game of it with a friend
► carrying your 'words for the day' on a scrap of paper in a pocket and consulting it at idle moments
► designing crosswords and word-searches for fellow-students
► memorising lists.

'Little and often' will result in a wide vocabulary.

Speaking

Knowledge of a foreign language is commonly described as 'speaking' it. And, as at GCSE, Speaking remains a major element in assessment of your performance at A-level (about 20 per cent). It is even more important at AS-level, where it may account for up to 40 per cent of the marks.

There is no doubt that, in the course of your A-level studies, you will come across a large amount of vocabulary and you will improve your knowledge of grammar. This really means that you ought to be speaking better German at the end of the two years.

For many students, however, this is not so. The main reason is quite simply lack of practice. There are, however, many ways of ensuring that you use the language.

1 Many teachers will run their classroom using German as the primary means of communication. You, as a student, will have to ask simple questions using phrases such as the following:

Ich verstehe das nicht.	*I don't understand.*
Können Sie das bitte wiederholen?	*Can you repeat that, please?*
Wie schreibt man das?	*How do you spell that?*
Was bedeutet 'Umweltschutz' auf deutsch/auf englisch?	*What does 'Umweltschutz' mean in German/in English?*
Ich habe leider meinen Kuli zu Hause liegenlassen.	*I'm afraid I have left my pen at home.*
Bis wann müssen wir die Aufgabe gemacht haben?	*When does the assignment have to be done by?*
Wann ist der Vokabeltest?	*When is the vocabulary test?*

2 Your teacher may ask you to define things in German, or to give examples or opposites in German. Don't miss this opportunity to practise speaking.
3 Take advantage of any 'warm-up spot' to the lesson where the teacher asks you for 'news' or recent events and doings.
4 You will find that your teacher asks you to discuss language topics in German. Many of these may be at least slightly controversial, and you will need to build a repertoire of debating phrases.
5 Some A-level syllabuses require you to write about literary works in German. Where this is so you may find yourself discussing the following in German:
   – what happened in a text
   – the motives of characters
   – your opinions of them.
This is quite tricky at first. But you can soon build a repertoire of suitable phrases to support your efforts, and you can often prepare what you have to say in advance.
6 If you are lucky enough to have a German Assistant, make the most of any time you have with him or her. It is an important part of your course. Consider inviting the Assistant to social events, too.
7 Do visit Germany if you get the chance. Inexpensive opportunities include an exchange, a twinning group, a sports club visit, staying in youth hostels (well established in German-speaking countries), using student Interrail cards (a good buy) or working holidays.

However you get practice in speaking German, be prepared to have a go at communicating. Of course accuracy matters at A-level. But there are always marks to be gained for keeping going or getting the message across and, in real life, these are the skills which will be most useful to you when using a foreign language.

Listening

As in Speaking, your abilities in Listening will have been assessed at GCSE. At A-level, too, there will be a test of Listening comprehension, worth about 20 per cent of the marks. At AS-level, it may be up to a third of the marks.

So, clearly you need to develop your listening comprehension skills. At first 'real' German, that is to say German spoken by native speakers to other native speakers, will seem impossibly fast. But with practice, by the end of your A-level or AS-level course, you ought to be able to follow a standard radio broadcast without much difficulty.

Here are a few suggestions for Listening activities and sources of material in German. But of course any of the activities suggested above for practising Speaking involve listening, too.

1   In class, you will hear your teacher, possibly the German Assistant, and almost certainly material recorded on audio cassette. As ever, the most productive way of listening is with a pen in your hand. With practice you will be able to write unknown words down well enough to ask about them afterwards, or to look them up in a dictionary.

2   You may be able to borrow or copy audio-cassette material you have heard in class. It will probably only be a few minutes long, and you will be able to make up a personal course tape which will help your revision.

3   With any recording, take a minute or so to make a transcript, using the rewind and pause buttons on your cassette machine or Walkman. Get someone competent to check it. You can do this yourself if you can find material which has a transcript, for example in a coursebook.

4   If you **can** find material with a transcript, use a photocopier to enlarge it and white out occasional words. You might ask someone else to do the whiting out for you. Then play the tape and use it to fill in the blanks.

5   Use the cassette which accompanies *Authentik* (for details see page 11). This has listening activities and a key. You may be able to borrow the cassette from your school or college.

6   If you have access to satellite TV you should be able to receive more than 16 German channels free. These include all the main German terrestial channels, as well as some material which is only on satellite. Occasional doses will do no harm, and may do some good. If you watch the news, it does have the advantage that you can find out what is being said by listening to a UK station.

7   As well as 'real' TV programmes, there is quite a good range of schools broadcasts available. Schools and colleges will have recorded series, and may be able to make them available to you. Even if the material is intended for beginners or near beginners, it will be beneficial in that it will reinforce what you already know and will contain some language which is more complex. TV titles to look for include *Lernexpress*, *Deutsch Direkt*, *Hallo aus Berlin*, *Treffpunkt Deutschland*, and *Treffpunkt Österreich*.

It is important to make sure that you have plenty of practice by listening to German, frequently, but in very small doses. You should try to cover a range of situations including:

- ▶ news broadcasts   ▶ stories
- ▶ weather forecasts   ▶ historical items
- ▶ traffic reports   ▶ humour.
- ▶ interviews

Revisit them often during your course. If you can do so, you will find that your competence increases steadily.

Writing

Writing correct German is the most demanding skill at A-level. The main difference between GCSE and A-level is that, while it is possible to get a high grade at GCSE without being more than reasonably good at writing, the same is not true of A-level.

Before the end of the first term of the A-level course you must be absolutely sure of the following:

- ► 40 strong verbs in present, perfect and imperfect
- ► weak verbs in present, perfect and imperfect
- ► adjective endings after *der* and *ein*
- ► the uses of the Nominative, Accusative, Dative and Genitive
- ► the common prepositions which
  - – always take Dative
  - – always take Accusative
  - – always take Genitive
  - – take either Dative or Accusative

All of the above can be looked up in a good reference grammar such as the *Longman A-level Study Guide German*.

Without a firm basis it is futile to attempt to master the more complicated grammar demanded by A-level.

The strategies given below will help you to improve your written work over your course and will also provide ideas for revision activities.

1 Write in German using alternate lines. This makes it easier for you to change things legibly after checking, and it is easier to write in corrections and alternative versions.

2 Prepare written work in rough, check it systematically and hand in a neat version that you believe to be correct. If the first draft, checking and writing up can be done on separate occasions, you will eliminate more errors and produce better work.

3 Checking is best done systematically with reference material to hand. One possible mode of proceeding is:

(a) Check genders
  (i) by applying gender rules
  (ii) by looking up individual words.

(b) Check cases
  (i) is there an Accusative after each verb?
  (ii) if not, do you know why?
  (iii) are the cases right after each preposition?

(c) Check adjectives
  (i) if they are not followed by a noun, they should not have an ending
  (ii) if they are followed by a noun, do they have the correct ending for
    – following *der*, *ein*, or no article?
    – the case of the noun?
    – the gender of the noun?
    – singular or plural?

(d) Check verbs
  (i) is the verb tense right in each instance?
  (ii) is the verb weak or strong?
  (iii) is the form of the verb right?
  (iv) does it need *haben* or *sein*?
  (v) does it agree with its subject?

(e) Check word order
  (i) is the verb in the right place? (second idea or at end of clause)
  (ii) are **time**, **manner**, **place** in that order?
  (iii) are DAN and PAD right (order of direct and indirect objects)?

(f) Check spelling
  (i) capital letters on nouns?
  (ii) *e* and *i* always the right way round?
  (iii) umlauts where needed?
  (iv) no umlauts over the letter *e* or *i*?
  (v) no words hyphenated over line ends?
  (vi) *ß* and *ss* correct?
  (vii) *sch* always with a *c*?

(g) Check punctuation
  (i) commas only for subordinate clauses and lists?
  (ii) speech marks in the right places?

4 Write out a fair copy of marked work which has been returned to you, incorporating the corrections and suggestions made. File it carefully with the original. This only takes a few minutes, but does draw your attention to the shortcomings.

5 Analyse the mistakes, note them, and act on preventing recurrence by looking up the point. If you can establish **what** it is that is causing you trouble, you are in a much better position to ask your teacher for help in dealing with it. Make the most of what are often relatively small teaching groups to get the individual help **you** require.

So, while practice certainly makes perfect in writing, analysis before, during and after writing makes perfect more quickly!

Reading

Finding German to read is not really a problem. And, given that Reading accounts for 20 per cent of many A-level syllabuses (more if you include the set texts in Literature/Civilisation options and the fact that some syllabuses set their Listening and Reading comprehension questions in German) and up to a third of AS-level syllabuses, you should aim to read a great deal of authentic German during your course.

Of course, merely turning the pages and letting the words roll over you will not help very much. What is needed is constructive reading, with something to show for it afterwards, and a programme which ensures you read a variety of text types.

You should be systematic in your approach to Reading. The following hints are likely to prove beneficial.

1 Always read with a pen and paper handy. You will approach reading more seriously seated on an upright chair at a desk. Note any vocabulary or phrase you had to look up, and anything which you understood readily, but which you might not perhaps have produced yourself.

2 File the notes you generate carefully, and keep a good record of what they refer to.

3 Particularly with newspaper and magazine articles, list synonyms which the writer has inserted to avoid repetition.

4 You could also decide to make a list of, say, the adverbs in a particular article, to extend your knowledge of them.

5 Every subject has its specialised vocabulary. Try listing what you have found on, for example, *die Umwelt*, and then compare it with a list prepared by someone else.

6 For magazine articles, try to discover the plan to which the article was written. Many will have an introduction, arguments for and against, and then a conclusion. Others may be more narrative. Many points will have a number of sub-points. Learning how to find them will make it easier to do summaries.

7 Try to be alive to nuances such as the use of the subjunctive to allow the writer to distance him- or herself from the opinions being expressed, or the use of adverbs such as *mutmaßlich* and *angeblich* to get round the libel laws.

8 Keep a record of your reading so you can see how many texts of a particular type you have read. From newspapers, include crime, politics, scandal, magazine sections, adverts, travel, reviews and human interest stories. You should also work through general interest articles in magazines such as *Brigitte* and in teenage magazines such as *Freundin*.

9 Obtaining German newspapers in Britain is not as difficult as you might think. In most large towns there will be a newsagent who stocks foreign newspapers. It is often a trader near the railway station.

10 As well as buying newspapers in Britain, you could perhaps ask someone who is travelling to Germany to pick some up for you. Frequently the contents of the pile of newsprint waiting to go to the *Altpapiersammlung* in most German households provide varied reading at no cost.

11 An excellent source of more structured journalistic material is the magazine *Authentik*. Published by Trinity College (27 Westland Square, Dublin 2, Eire, Tel: 00 353 16 771512), it is a digest of a variety of publications, often with exercises. It represents an excellent buy for A-level students. A cassette containing linked audio material is available with each issue.

Finding German to read is not difficult. Active reading ensures that none of the effort involved is wasted. If you stick at it, it will be among the first areas of the course where you can really feel the progress you are making.

Literature, Civilisation and coursework

The Literature and/or Civilisation component of A-level is a new element of language study. You may have been quite apprehensive about this new area of work, but there is nothing magical about it. In the main, much of the value of this part of the course is that it extends your skill of reading comprehension and, where exam candidates have to write their answers in German, your skill of arguing and writing in German.

What many students find worrying is having to write essays either as answers to examination questions or – at greater length – as coursework if they are taking that option. Both sorts of essay mean you will be able to use your skills of planning, drafting and perhaps redrafting to produce a really polished piece of work, which can be very satisfying.

The first distinction to be made is between essays done during the A-level course, which are part of the learning process, and those done in limited time under examination conditions and with few or no reference materials.

1 **Essays done during your course** are meant to get you to look at particular problems fully. You should expect to spend a good number of hours researching, planning, drafting and writing each one, using a methodical approach. If you do this, you will have a good source of information, produced to a high standard, to revise from later. When the essay has been marked, do some more work to see how the notes you have and the conclusions you have reached can be improved. This will allow you to have a really polished version available for revision.

2 The **exam essay** is a different thing entirely. Your aim is to communicate in, say 45 minutes, that:
   - you know a text or topic well
   - you can express and justify your opinion
   - you can muster arguments in response to the problem posed in the title.

Exam essays will necessarily be much shorter than an essay written while you are 'learning' a topic, but will have a very clear logic which is easy for the examiner to follow. The essay should be legible. Write on alternate lines so that, if you need to change or add something, you have space to do it clearly.

Good preparation for the A-level examination, therefore, will include practice at turning 'learning' essays into timed examination pieces. Even if your teacher does not provide the chance for you to do this in class, you can do it at home. One advantage is that such a task has to be completed in 45–60 minutes.

Structure and planning
A good essay:

► answers the question
► has a clear structure
► has evidence to back up each assertion made
► considers other points of view
► comes to an obvious conclusion or makes it clear why no conclusion can be drawn.

Steps in planning

1   Read the question carefully   Remember: If all else fails, read the question!
Questions may include such phrases as :

Inwiefern...   *To what extent...*
Besprechen Sie...   *Discuss...*
Beschreiben Sie...   *Describe...*
Diskutieren Sie...   *Discuss...*
Nehmen Sie Stellung zu dieser Aussage.   *Give your opinion on this statement.*
Vergleichen Sie...   *Compare...*
Wie stehen Sie dazu?   *What is your opinion?*

Bear in mind that if the question asks you to discuss the significance of something,
and you hardly mention it, you are unlikely to score high marks. So read questions
carefully, **especially** in the heat of the examination.

If the question consists of a quotation or a statement which you are asked to
discuss, you have the option of agreeing or disagreeing. You will get the same
marks whichever approach you choose, providing you can support your point of
view. If you are asked to write an appreciation of a work of literature or an insti-
tution, it is more difficult to do a 'demolition job' than to sing its praises.

One technique which can be helpful is to take a phrase or a word out of the
title and use it several times in your essay. This helps to keep you from getting off
the point.

Another technique for preventing 'waffling' is to ask a question and answer it in
each paragraph. If the question refers back to the title, so much the better.

The major pitfall to be avoided in answers about set books is to retell the story
without making any real attempt to answer the question. What is being sought is
your ability to analyse the topic in the title with reference to the text.

Another feature of weak candidates' literature answers is that they preface their
remarks with lengthy details about the author's upbringing and his or her times.
For a very few questions this may be relevant. But for most, it simply does not
answer the question set.

2   Make the structure clear   Many students find planning an essay difficult. If
you can't think where to begin, try brainstorming. Write down a brief reference to
everything you can think of in answer to the essay title on a piece of paper. On
another piece of paper rewrite them in some kind of order, crossing them off on
the original as you go. You may have to try this more than once until you get a sat-
isfactory order. Different-coloured pens can be used to cheer the whole process up.

Your structure may follow one of the following patterns (the suggested percent-
ages of length are for guidance only):

(a) **for and against**

Introduction	10%
For	40%
Against	40%
Conclusion	10%

(b) **analysis of features**

Introduction	10%
Feature A	
Feature B	80%
Feature C (etc.)	
Conclusion	10%

(c) **compare or contrast**

Introduction	10%
X's Feature A compared with Y's Feature A	
X's Feature B compared with Y's Feature B	} 80%
X's Feature C compared with Y's Feature C (etc.)	
Conclusion	10%

(d) **development**

Introduction	10%
Change/Event/Development A	
Change/Event/Development B	} 80%
Change/Event/Development C (etc.)	
Conclusion	10%

It is also good practice to 'flag' the various parts of your structure by beginning each paragraph with such phrases as:

Besprechen wir zuerst die Argumente für...	*Let us first discuss the arguments for...*
Jetzt kommen wir zu den Gegenargumenten	*Now we come to the arguments against*
Xs Wortwahl ist kennzeichnend für sein Werk.	*X's choice of language is typical of his work.*
Nachdem Y etabliert war, entstand eine Nachfrage nach Z.	*After Y had been established, a demand for Z arose.*
Zum Schluß scheint es eindeutig, daß...	*In conclusion, it seems clear that...*

3 **Give evidence for what you say**   Evidence for the opinions you express must be given. This can be done:

- by alluding to something, e.g. 'as X's hurried return to Berlin by train shows'
- by using a relevant quotation, e.g. '*seine* **übereilte** *Rückkehr nach Berlin*'
- by referring briefly to something, e.g. 'X's hasty return'.

It is important to have evidence for every statement to show that you have knowledge of the text or the topic, and that you have thought about the significance of each piece of information.

4 **Consider other points of view**   Even though you may have very clear views on a subject, academic practice demands that you show you understand the opposite point of view and are able to explain clearly the reasons for not accepting it.

5 **Come to an obvious conclusion or make it clear why no conclusion can be drawn**   Either come down in favour of one side or other of an argument, or state clearly that no conclusion is possible and say why. In some types of essay, your conclusion can be a summary of the features and development followed by an opinion.

Preparing and presenting coursework

Much of what has been said about tackling examination essays applies to coursework. To recap, the extended essay should share the characteristics of a good essay, i.e. it should:

▶ answer the question
▶ have a clear structure

▶ have evidence proving each assertion made

▶ consider other points of view

▶ come to an obvious conclusion or make it clear why no conclusion can be drawn.

Because coursework can be checked, however, it is expected to contain fewer errors than work written under examination conditions. Where coursework is written in German, it should be subjected to careful checking, as outlined above (see page 9). If you word-process it, you should try and find a program which has the umlaut and *ß*. No allowance is made for typing errors – they remain errors. See page 4 for further advice on using a word-processor.

Examiners are concerned that candidates should:

▶ give evidence of commitment and personal intellectual input

▶ write in accurate German

▶ base their work on material which originated in Germany

▶ include quotations but make sure they are relevant

▶ include a title sheet and bibliography

▶ write with plenty of space round their work

▶ stick fairly accurately to the word-count given.

Revision

Revision planning

Being organised produces better results. This applies, of course, to revision as well as to normal study. Here are the key features of efficient revision:

1 **Know how long you have left**   Work out how many weeks there are before the examination by counting the weeks on a calendar. For A-level German, the various examinations are spread over several weeks, so time the run-up to each one individually. There is little point in working on Reading the day before your Speaking test, for example.

2 **Plan your revision**   This should be done week by week, topic by topic, skill by skill. Allow a week near the end for 'slippage' – time to catch up on what you have missed. Don't be overambitious about what you can get done. You may need to prioritise your efforts in areas you know are weak.

3 **Know what to expect in the exam**   Check the exact details with your teacher. Knowing what to expect gives direction and urgency to your revision and prevents you wasting time on irrelevant material.

4 **Check you can do it**   Make sure you can do all the obvious things such as plan a coherent essay, etc.

5 **Spot questions**   Use the sample and past papers available for A-level German to find out the sort of things that come up.

6 **Analyse your own performance**   Use your mock examination to work out where your weaknesses are, and do something about them. If necessary, consult your teacher who, after all, knows your abilities best – and take his or her advice. Your teacher will probably have seen dozens of A-level candidates over the years and will know what needs doing. You, on the other hand, are doing the examination for the first time.

Planned revision pays off. **Revise early and revise often!**

Revision techniques

Revision can be boring because, by definition, you have seen things you are revising before. You need to find ways of compensating for the lack of novelty.

Many students revise ineffectively because they merely read through notes and chapters in their files and let the information wash over them. This is almost always a waste of time, certainly after the first half-hour or so. The secret is to **do** something, because activity is an aid to concentration.

German is a skills-based subject and you will improve your performance by practice. Any good musician or sporting star will confirm that the best forms of practice contain variety.

Useful techniques include the following:

1 Write notes Make yourself skeleton notes which are sufficiently detailed to jog your memory, perhaps on small pieces of card (index cards or chopped up pieces of cereal packet). You can carry these about with you and consult them in odd moments. With vocabulary, write nouns down with their gender, plural and meaning to help to fix them in your memory. Alternatively, write down a phrase which contains the word and its gender. If you are reading German, make a note of every word you had to look up.

2 Work with a friend Pick a friend who is about the same standard as you are, and who also wants to work. Testing each other is a good idea. But don't forget to include written testing, which is the real proof of whether you know things. Because of the danger of being side-tracked by friends, don't rely on this method of revision alone.

3 Set yourself tests While learning, make a note of things you found hard and test yourself later – at the end of your session, then the following day, then the following week. Be honest with yourself about how you got on!

4 Tick off what you've done Using the revision plan you have made, tick off the topics you have dealt with. Again, be honest! The more you have dealt with, the better you will feel.

5 Set realistic targets Doing too much in one session will cause frustration and depress you. It is much better to learn, say, ten irregular verbs and succeed than to try to learn 56 and fail miserably.

6 Treat yourself After a reasonable stint of revision, give yourself a treat – a sweet, a break or the chance to watch a favourite soap opera. Give yourself short-term incentives.

7 Don't work too long without a break 45–50 minutes is probably the longest session most people can concentrate for without a break – even if it's only to stretch your legs for five minutes.

8 Give yourself variety Vary the aspects you revise. Also, vary the subjects you do in any one session – three spells of 45–50 minutes on three different subjects will be more productive than a three-hour 'slog' on one subject.

9 Ignore other students Some fellow-students will be loudly proclaiming either that they 'never do any revision' or that they are 'up working till 2 a.m.' Ignore them. They are being hysterical, and may well be embroidering the truth anyway. What matters to you is not how much or how little revision your friends do, but how much **you** do.

10 Know when you are not revising Don't kid yourself that you are working when you aren't. No one can revise effectively while watching TV, chatting to friends, washing their hair or eating a meal. Don't even attempt it. Use these activities to reward yourself **after** a revision session.

The examination

Examination techniques

The best cure for examination nerves is knowing that you have done all reasonable preparation. In addition, there are various practical things you can do to make sure you can concentrate on the examination paper.

The evening before an examination

▶ Pack your bag and put it by the front door to eliminate last-minute panic. Include spare pens, pencils and rubbers, your dictionary, and a silent watch.

▶ At the end of the evening, relax by doing something other than work. If you can manage to take the whole evening off, that's even better.

▶ Go to bed at a reasonable hour so you have enough sleep.

The morning before an examination

▶ Get up in good time to avoid rush and panic.

▶ Dress carefully, possibly even smartly, to take your mind off the examination.

▶ Eat a reasonable breakfast so you aren't hungry during the examination.

Just before the examination

▶ Be there in good time, but not **too** early.

▶ Read or listen to something **easy** and familiar in German.

In the exam room

▶ Sit as comfortably as possible. To stop your desk rocking, use folded paper.

▶ Make sure you know which options you have entered for in the skill being tested, and that you have been given the right paper.

▶ Check the number of questions you have to answer and the time available. Divide up your time and write down 'clock times' for each question.

▶ Read the questions carefully. You may need to consult a dictionary.

▶ Do the tasks you are asked to do.

▶ Pace yourself so you have enough time to answer the more difficult questions at the end of the paper. If you can't do a question early in the paper quickly, leave it and come back to it later.

▶ Don't leave blanks – make a sensible guess. This applies especially to multiple-choice and tick-box questions.

▶ Use your common sense in Listening and Reading papers. If you don't know what happened, think what a sane and rational person might do in identical circumstances. Logic applies equally in the German-speaking world.

▶ When you have finished, check your work systematically.

▶ In Reading and Listening examinations, have you given enough details?

▶ In Writing examinations, check verbs, genders and agreements.

▶ Ignore the behaviour of other candidates. Many poor candidates demonstratively sit back or go to sleep having 'finished', or even walk out early. Don't be tempted to imitate them.

▶ After the Speaking test avoid panicking others by saying how terrible it was, etc. Smile sweetly and wish them good luck.

▶ When it's all over celebrate moderately.

Grammar problems

Introduction

Many students find writing accurate German a problem. In the study skills chapter we have suggested strategies for checking written work (see page 9). This chapter provides quick reference for some of the more common grammatical points which, in our experience, cause the majority of problems for A-level students. It is not, however, a full reference grammar. A complete reference grammar for A-level can be found in the *Longman A-level Study Guide German*.

Adjectives

> **HINT**
> Students also learning French sometimes make adjectives standing alone agree, as they do in French. This is **wrong**.

In German adjectives may or may not agree with (change their spelling to match) the noun they describe.

Adjectives not followed by a noun

Adjectives which stand alone – usually after *sein*, *werden* and *scheinen* – do not have an adjective ending.

Example
Die Frau ist **groß**   *The woman is tall*

Adjectives followed by a noun

Adjectives followed by a noun take an ending (= agree with the noun) which depends on four factors:

1 the determiner (article) or lack of one in front of the adjective
2 the gender of the noun – masculine, feminine, or neuter
3 whether the noun is singular or plural
4 the case of the noun.

If there is more than one adjective before the noun, each one has the appropriate ending. Of course, once one ending has been worked out, all the others in front of the same noun will have the same ending.

   There are three sets of adjective endings, depending on which determiner is used. They are laid out in Tables 1–3.

Table 1   After *der/die/das*, etc.; *dieser*; *jener*; *jeder*; *welcher*; *solcher*; *mancher*; and *alle* (which is, of course, plural)

	Masculine singular	*Feminine singular*	*Neuter singular*	*Plural, all genders*
Nom.	der groß**e** Mann	die groß**e** Frau	das groß**e** Kind	die groß**en** Leute
Acc.	den groß**en** Mann	die groß**e** Frau	das groß**e** Kind	die groß**en** Leute
Gen.	des groß**en** Mann**es**	der groß**en** Frau	des groß**en** Kind**es**	der groß**en** Leute
Dat.	dem groß**en** Mann(**e**)	der groß**en** Frau	dem groß**en** Kind(**e**)	den groß**en** Leuten

> **HINT** ▶ *All Genitive and Dative singular and all plural endings are -en.*
> ▶ *Note that -es or -s is usually added to masculine and neuter nouns in the Genitive singular.*

► Note that -e can be added to single-syllable masculine and neuter nouns in the Dative singular in formal writing.
► Remember to add -n to nouns which do not already have one in the Dative plural of all genders, unless the plural ends in -s.

Table 2 After *ein/eine/ein*, etc.; *kein*; *mein, dein, sein, ihr* (=her), *seine, unser, euer, Ihr* and *ihr* (=their)

	Masculine singular	*Feminine singular*	*Neuter singular*	*Plural, all genders*
Nom.	ein groß**er** Mann	eine groß**e** Frau	ein groß**es** Kind	keine groß**en** Leute
Acc.	einen groß**en** Mann	eine groß**e** Frau	ein groß**es** Kind	keine groß**en** Leute
Gen.	eines groß**en** Mann**es**	einer groß**en** Frau	eines groß**en** Kind**es**	keiner groß**en** Leute
Dat.	einem groß**en** Mann(**e**)	einer groß**en** Frau	einem groß**en** Kind(**e**)	keinen groß**en** Leute**n**

HINT Ein *itself, for reasons of logic, doesn't have a plural. If 'a' is plural (i.e. 'some' – einige), it follows the plural pattern for Table 3, below.*

Table 3 Adjectives which are used alone before the noun

	Masculine singular	*Feminine singular*	*Neuter singular*	*Plural, all genders**
Nom.	kalt**er** Kaffee	kalt**e** Milch	kalt**es** Wasser	kalt**e** Getränke
Acc.	kalt**en** Kaffee	kalt**e** Milch	kalt**es** Wasser	kalt**e** Getränke
Gen.	kalt**en** Kaffee**s**	kalt**er** Milch	kalt**en** Wasser**s**	kalt**er** Getränke
Dat.	kalt**em** Kaffee	kalt**er** Milch	kalt**em** Wasser	kalt**en** Getränke**n**

(*also after *viele, mehrere, einige, ein paar* and numbers)

HINT *In the Genitive singular for masculine and neuter, the ending is -en, which might just seem a little unexpected.*

Adjectives used as nouns
All adjectives and participles can be used as nouns in German. They are then written with a capital letter.

Example
der Deutsche/die Deutsche   *the German*

Adjective-type nouns take the same endings as they would if they were followed by a noun of the appropriate gender.

Examples

Masculine singular	*Feminine singular*	*Plural*
Table 1		
der Angestellt**e**	die Angestellt**e**	die Angestellt**en**
den Angestellt**en**	die Angestellt**e**	die Angestellt**en**
des Angestellt**en**	der Angestellt**en**	der Angestellt**en**
dem Angestellt**en**	der Angestellt**en**	den Angestellt**en**
Table 2		
ein Angestellt**er**	eine Angestellt**e**	Angestellt**e**
einen Angestellt**en**	eine Angestellt**e**	Angestellt**e**
eines Angestellt**en**	einer Angestellt**en**	Angestellt**er**
einem Angestellt**en**	einer Angestellt**en**	Angestellt**en**

Something and nothing

After *etwas* (something) and *nichts* (nothing) the adjective is written with a capital letter and has *-es* added.

Examples
etwas **Gutes**   *something good*
nichts **Schlechtes**   *nothing bad*

Cases

The four cases in German are one of the principal areas of difficulty for English-speaking learners. Here are the basic rules for their use:

Nominative

The Nominative is used:

1 for the subject of a verb

Examples
Ich heiße Egon   *My name is Egon*
Heute schmeckte **der Fisch** ausgezeichnet   *The fish was excellent today*

2 after the verbs *sein, werden, bleiben, heißen* and *scheinen* and after the passive of *nennen*

Examples
Du bist und bleibst **mein Lieblingsvetter**   *You are and remain my favourite cousin*
Er scheint **ein wunderbarer Fußballer**   *He seems a wonderful footballer*
Karl I. wurde **Karl der Große** genannt   *Charles I was called Charlemagne*

3 in exclamations, when addressing people and where there is no obvious reason for any other case

Examples
Was hast du, **alter Freund**?   *What's the matter, old friend?*

Accusative

The Accusative is used:

1 for the direct object (the thing that suffers the action of the verb) of active, transitive verbs

Example
Ich habe **den Mann** gesehen   *I saw the man*

2 after certain prepositions. Some of them may take the Dative in certain circumstances (see 'Prepositions' on page 24).
3 for expressions of definite time

Examples
nächste Woche   *next week*
Es hat **den ganzen Monat** geregnet   *It rained all month*
Donnerstag, **den 17. August 1999**   *Thursday 17 August 1999*

4 for greetings and wishes

Examples
Herzlichen Glückwunsch!   *Congratulations!*
Guten Abend!   *Good evening!*

Genitive
The Genitive is used:

1 to denote 'of' or possession

Examples
Das Auto **meiner Eltern**   *My parents' car*
Das Dach **des Hauses**   *The roof of the house*

Note: Von + *Dative is used increasingly in preference to the Genitive, particularly to avoid a series of Genitives.*

Example
Er guckte durch das Fenster **vom Hause** des Lehrers   *He looked through the window of the teacher's house*

2 with the names of people, towns or countries an alternative form similar to English usage is found (the Saxon Genitive)

Example
Frau Krechels Mercedes   *Frau Krechel's Mercedes*

3 to show indefinite time

Examples
eines schönen Sommertages   *one fine summer's day*

4 after certain prepositions (see 'Prepositions' on page 24)

> **HINT**
> There is **no** apostrophe in German.

Dative
The Dative is used:

1 for the indirect object of a verb

Example
Er gab **dem Mann** das Buch   *He gave the book to the man*

2 after certain prepositions. Some of them may take the Accusative in certain circumstances (see 'Prepositions' on page 24).
3 after certain verbs which always take the Dative (see 'Verbs' on page 28)
4 to express advantage or disadvantage for someone

Examples
Sie kaufte **ihm** eine Banane   *She bought a banana for him/ She bought him a banana*
Man hat **mir** meinen Wagen gestohlen   *They stole my car from me*

5 in certain impersonal constructions expressing sensations

Examples
Mir ist warm   *I am hot*
Ihm wurde übel   *He felt sick*

> **HINT**
> Beware of missing the Dative, which is not always obvious from the English. This example could be translated as: He gave the man the book.

Comparisons

Adverbs and adjectives can be used in comparative (e.g. bigger, faster) and superlative (e.g. biggest, fastest) forms.
  In German, the principle is much the same.

Examples
schnell   *fast*
schnell**er**   *faster*
der/die/das schnell**ste***   *the fastest*
am schnellsten   *in the fastest manner*
* takes the same endings as any other adjective

Comparative sentence patterns

Note the ways of expressing positive and negative comparisons.

Examples
Ich bin aber intelligenter **als** du   *But I am more intelligent than you*
Ich bin **nicht so** intelligent **wie** Albert Einstein   *I am not as intelligent as Albert Einstein*

Superlative sentence patterns

Examples
Ich spiele **am besten** Tennis   *I play tennis best of all*
Ich bin **der beste** (Tennisspieler)   *I am the best (tennis player)*
Das wäre **am besten**   *That would be best*

Common irregular comparative and superlative forms

1   A number of common adjectives form comparatives in the usual way, but add an umlaut.

Examples
arm   *poor*
ärmer   *poorer*
der ärmste   *the poorest*

These include:

alt *old*	kalt *cold*	scharf *sharp*
dumm *stupid*	klug *clever*	schwach *weak*
groß *large*	krank *ill*	schwarz *black*
hart *hard*	kurz *short*	stark *strong*
jung *young*	lang *long*	warm *warm*

2   Some adjectives and adverbs have very irregular comparative and superlative forms.

bald	eher	am ehesten	*soon*
gern	lieber	am liebsten	*willingly*
gut	besser	der beste	*good*
hoch	höher	der höchste	*high*
nah	näher	der nächste	*near*
oft	öfter/häufiger	am häufigsten	*frequently*
viel	mehr	der meiste	*much, most*

Nouns

Gender

Knowing which nouns are grammatically masculine, feminine or neuter is difficult for English-speaking learners. The best way of learning which is which is to note down the gender and plural form of each noun you come across. However, there are a few simple rules which relate gender to the form of the noun.

Masculine by form
Nouns with the following endings are masculine (plural forms are given in brackets):

Ending	Example	
-ant (en)	der Passant	*passer-by*
-ig (e)	der König	*king*
-or (en)	der Motor	*engine*

-ast (e)	der Kontrast	*contrast*
-ismus (no pl.)	der Kommunismus	*communism*
-us (-en)	der Rhythmus	*rhythm*
-ich (e)	der Teppich	*carpet, rug*
-ling (e)	der Liebling	*darling*

Feminine by form
Nouns with the following endings are feminine:

Ending	**Example**	
-a (-en)	die Villa (die Villen)	*villa*
-anz (no pl.)	die Eleganz	*elegance*
-ei (en)	die Bücherei	*library*
-enz (en)	die Tendenz	*tendency*
-heit (en)	die Freiheit	*freedom*
-ie (n)	die Technologie	*technology*
-ik (en)	die Musik	*music*
-in (nen)	die Lehrerin	*female teacher*
-keit (en)	die Freundlichkeit	*friendliness*
-schaft (en)	die Freundschaft	*friendship*
-sion (en)	die Explosion	*explosion*
-sis (-sen)	die Basis (die Basen)	*basis*
-tion (en)	die Situation	*situation*
-tät (en)	die Aktivität	*activity*
-ung (en)	die Landung	*landing (on beach)*

Exceptions: das Sofa, der Papagei (*parrot*), das Genie (*genius*), der Atlantik, der Katholik, das Mosaik, der Pazifik

Neuter by form
Nouns with the following endings are neuter:

Ending	**Example**	
-chen (-)	das Mädchen	*girl*
-icht (e)	das Dickicht	*thicket*
-il (e)	das Krokodil	*crocodile*
-lein	das Fräulein	*miss, young lady*
-ment (s)	das Appartement	*apartment*
-tel	das Zehntel	*tenth*
-tum (no pl.)	das Christentum	*Christianity*

Compound words
These take the gender and the plural of the last part.

Examples

der Stundenplan (-pläne) *timetable*
die Straßenbahnhaltestelle (n) *tram stop*
das Freibad (-bäder) *open air swimming pool*

Unhelpful genders of names of human beings

die Geisel (n) *hostage*
das Genie (s) *genius*
das Individuum (Individuen) *individual*
das Mädchen (-) *girl*
das Mitglied (er) *member*

die Person (en) *person*
das Weib (er) *woman*

Plural forms

Where the ending of a noun determines the gender, as listed above, plurals are always as listed. For other nouns, the only guaranteed way to make real progress in learning plural forms is to note them with each new word.

Spelling changes in nouns

German nouns have slight spelling changes in the following circumstances:

1 In the Genitive singular, masculine and neuter nouns add an -*s*, or, if single-syllable words, often -*es*.

Example
wegen des starken Wind**es** *because of the strong wind*
trotz des Regen**s** *despite the rain*

2 In the Dative plural, irrespective of gender, an -*n* is added if one is not already present, unless the plural ends in -*s*.

Example
mit den Schüler**n** *with the school students*

Weak nouns

These nouns are slightly irregular. All but one of them *(das Herz)* are masculine.

1 The majority have -*en* throughout the plural and in all cases of the singular except the Nominative. They do **not** have an -*s* in the Genitive singular:

Examples

	Singular	Plural
Nom.	der Schotte	die Schotten
Acc.	den Schotten	die Schotten
Gen.	des Schotten	der Schotten
Dat.	dem Schotten	den Schotten

	Singular	Plural
der Mensch	die Menschen
den Menschen	die Menschen
des Menschen	der Menschen
dem Menschen	den Menschen

They include the following categories of nouns:

(a) those ending in -*e* in the Nominative singular (which is how they are listed in the dictionary)

Examples
der Affe *monkey*, der Bursche *lad*, der Franzose *Frenchman*

Exceptions: *der Käse* and the eight nouns listed in **2**

(b) some German-root nouns not ending in -*e* in the Nominative singular

These include:

der Bär *bear*	der Herr *gentleman*
der Bauer *peasant*	der Hirt *shepherd*
der Bayer *Bavarian*	der Mensch *human being*
der Fürst *prince*	der Nachbar *neighbour*
der Fotograf *photographer*	der Narr *fool*
der Held *hero*	der Untertan *subject (of monarch)*

HINT
Weak nouns are common. Make sure you know at least ten of them in all four cases.

(c) foreign nouns ending in *-and, -ant, -aph, -arch, -at, -ent, -et, -ist, -krat, -log, -nom, -on*

    Examples

der Konfirmand	*confirmation candidate*	der Komet	*comet*
der Ministrant	*server (in church)*	der Organist	*organist*
der Seraph	*seraph*	der Autokrat	*autocrat*
der Monarch	*monarch*	der Astrolog	*astrologer*
der Automat	*robot, slot machine*	der Astronom	*astronomer*
der Student	*student (university)*	der Dämon	*demon*

(d) some other foreign words:

der Barbar	*barbarian*	der Katholik	*Catholic*
der Chirurg	*surgeon*	der Tyrann	*tyrant*
der Kamarad	*comrade, friend*		

2 Eight masculine nouns behave like those in **1**, except that they have *-ens* in the Genitive singular.

Example:

	Singular	Plural
Nom.	der Name	die Namen
Acc.	den Namen	die Namen
Gen.	des Namens	der Namen
Dat.	dem Namen	den Namen

The other seven are:

der Buchstabe	*letter of the alphabet*	der Glaube	*belief*
der Friede	*peace*	der Same	*seed*
der Funke	*spark*	der Wille	*will*
der Gedanke	*thought*		

3 *das Herz* is declined like this:

	Singular	Plural
Nom.	das Herz	die Herzen
Acc.	das Herz	die Herzen
Gen.	des Herzens	der Herzen
Dat.	dem Herzen	den Herzen

Prepositions

Prepositions express a relationship between one noun and another, often of position. In German prepositions are followed by different cases. For the majority of prepositions, it is merely a matter of knowing what they 'take' ('govern'). For example, *mit* takes the Dative. However, there is a group of common prepositions which take either Accusative or Dative according to their meaning.

    Mastering the use of at least the common prepositions is one of the essential – but tricky – jobs of the A-level student. It really is worth committing the lists of the common prepositions and the case(s) they take to memory. We have listed just the common prepositions for convenience.

Prepositions which always take the Accusative

bis   *as far as; until*
durch   *through; throughout; by*
für   *for*
gegen   *against; towards; in exchange for; about; compared with*
ohne   *without*
um   *round; about; at + clock times; concerning; by (degree of difference)*

Prepositions which always take the Dative

ab   *from*
aus   *out of; made of*
außer   *except for; out of (use)*
bei   *by; at; at the house of; in view of; on the occasion of*
gegenüber*   *opposite; compared with; in relation to; towards*
mit   *with; by*
nach   *to; towards; after + time; according to*
seit   *since; for (uses a more recent tense than in English)*
von   *from; by; of*
zu   *to; (sometimes) at; for; as; towards; at + price*
* may precede or follow the noun

> **HINT** ► Aus *and* zu *both look as though they might take the Accusative because they imply motion (see below). They* **never** *take the Accusative.*
>
> ► *In the Dative plural, most nouns add an -n if they do not already have one. It's easy to forget it.*

Prepositions which take either Accusative or Dative

Ten common prepositions take either Accusative or Dative. Two basic rules apply to the majority of instances:

1 If the preposition expresses position, then the Dative is used. If it expresses motion in relation to, the Accusative is used.

Example
Ich gehe in die Stadt (in + Accusative – motion)   *I go into town*
Ich wohne in der Stadt (in + Dative – position)   *I live in the town*

This can lead to fine distinctions. The movement is relative to the noun.

Contrast: Ich gehe **ins** Zimmer   *I walk into the room*
              (I start outside the room and finish up inside it, so motion has occurred)
with: Ich gehe **im** Zimmer herum   *I walk around in the room*
              (I start walking inside the room and finish walking inside the room, so no motion relative to the room has occurred)

Verbs of arriving, appearing and disappearing are usually used in conjunction with a Dative.

Example
Ich bin **am Bahnhof** angekommen   *I arrived at the station*

2 If the preposition expresses a figurative sense, it often takes the Accusative.

Example
Er weiß viel **über die Stadt**   *He knows a lot about the town*

Although the above rules can apply to most of the Accusative/Dative prepositions, in practice the majority of them are most frequently found in the cases indicated in brackets. It is really *an, auf, in* and *über* which most often require careful thought. *Follows the noun.

an   *on (the side of); at; of*
auf   *on (top of); at; in*
entlang* (usually + Acc)   *along*
hinter (usually + Dat)   *behind*
in   *in; inside*
neben (usually + Dat)   *next to*
über   *over; about; more than*
unter (usually + Dat)   *under; below; among*

vor (usually + Dat)   *in front of; before*
zwischen (usually + Dat)   *between*

Prepositions which take the Genitive
anstatt   *instead of*
statt   *instead of*
trotz   *despite, in spite of*
während   *during*
wegen   *because of*

Pronouns

Pronouns stand in the place of a noun, and are used to avoid repetition. The case is determined by the pronoun's function in the sentence. Many pronoun usages are relatively straightforward. However, make sure that you are **not** one of the candidates who cannot spell *man* or *wir*.

Er, sie and es

1   'It' may refer to a masculine or feminine noun and in German *er* or *sie*, *ihn* or *sie*, *ihm* or *ihr* may be required. *Er* and *sie* do not refer solely to biological gender.

Examples
Hier ist die Banane. Ich habe **sie** gestern gekauft   *Here is the banana. I bought it yesterday*
Hier ist der berühmte Wagen. Ich bin mit **ihm** zum Nordkapp gefahren   *Here is the famous car. I drove it to North Cape*

2   There is occasional conflict between biological and grammatical gender, particularly with *das Mädchen* and *das Fräulein*. They can be referred to as either *es* or *sie*.

3   After prepositions, special rules apply:
(a) *Es* is never used after a preposition. Instead the preposition has the prefix *da(r)* attached to give *darauf*, *danach*, etc.

Examples
Hier ist endlich das Schiff. Wir haben lang genug darauf gewartet   *Here is the ship at last. We've been waiting for it long enough*

(b) Where **people** are referred to, the normal forms of the pronouns are used after prepositions.

Example
Bist du mit ihr gekommen?   *Did you come with her?*

Relative pronouns

A major area of difficulty is relative pronouns. Relative pronouns correspond to *who, whom, whose, which* or *that* in English.

HINT *It is important to know the test for whether 'that' is in fact a relative pronoun or best translated by* daß. *If 'who' or 'which' can be substituted for 'that' without changing the meaning, it is a relative pronoun. If the substitution cannot be made without generating nonsense, use* daß.

Examples
This is the house that Jack built
Substitute 'which':
This is the house which Jack built
Therefore the original 'that' is a relative pronoun.

I think that you should go
Substitute 'which':
I think which you should go
This is nonsense, and 'that' should be *daß*.

A further complication is that the relative pronoun is often missed out in English, in such sentences as: *This is the book I am reading at the moment*. This **never** happens in German.

The form of the relative pronoun

	Masculine	**Feminine**	**Neuter**	**Plural**	**Meaning**
Nom.	der	die	das	die	*who, which, that*
Acc.	den	die	das	die	*who(m), which, that*
Gen.	dessen	deren	dessen	deren	*whose, of which*
Dat.	dem	der	dem	denen	*to whom, to which*

Agreement
The relative pronoun agrees with the noun to which it refers in number (singular or plural) and gender (masculine, feminine or neuter), but **not** in case. The case of the relative pronoun is determined by its function in the relative clause.

Case
If the suggested English translations of the relative pronoun are borne in mind, it is quite possible to sort out which case to choose.

Examples
                    Nom.
Ich bin eine Lehrerin, **die** oft nach Deutschland fährt   *I am a teacher **who/that** often travels to Germany*

                    Acc.
Ich bin ein Lehrer, **den** man oft in der Stadt sieht   *I am a teacher (**that/who/whom**) you can often see in town*

                    Gen.
Ich bin ein Mann, **dessen** Kinder artig sind   *I am a man **whose** children are well-behaved*

                    Dat.
Seefahrer sind Leute, **mit denen** ich nichts anfangen kann   *Seamen are people **with whom** I don't get on*

Was
After *alles*, *nichts*, *etwas*, and the less frequent *einiges, folgendes, manches* and *vieles*, the relative pronoun is always *was*.

Example
Alles, **was** ich habe, ist mein Hund   *All I have is my dog*

Das, was
Note the idiomatic use of *das, was* :

Example
Ich habe nur **das, was** ich mitgebracht habe   *I only have what (that which) I have brought with me*

HINT *In German the punctuation rules require that relative pronouns have a comma in front of them. This is unlike many English relative clauses – beware!*

Verbs

Weak, strong and mixed verbs

In German there are two sorts of verbs, regular (i.e. those which follow a rule) and irregular (i.e. those which do not always follow a rule and which therefore have to be learnt).

Regular verbs are often referred to as **weak** verbs in German, perhaps because they do not have a mind of their own.

Irregular German verbs are often referred to as **strong** verbs, perhaps because they are strong-minded.

In any dictionary there is an overwhelming majority of weak verbs. However, in any lengthy piece of German there is probably a majority of strong verbs, which often express common actions.

Some dictionaries and grammars refer to **mixed verbs**. These are verbs which are irregular, but share some of the characteristics of weak verbs. Despite that, they are still irregular, and need to be specially learnt.

When a verb is listed in a dictionary, it is given in the infinitive.

Example
spielen　*to play*
fahren　*to travel*

For the formation of tenses, the infinitive will normally be the starting point.

How to read a verb table

Irregular verbs are listed in verb tables. Typical entries might look like this:

Infinitive	3rd person present	Imperfect	Past participle	Imperfect subjunctive	Meaning
essen	ißt	aß	gegessen	ässe	eat
fahren	fährt	fuhr	gefahren(*)	führe	travel, drive
gehen		ging	gegangen*	ginge	go
haben		hatte	gehabt	hätte	have

The **infinitive** is the verb as listed in the dictionary. The meaning is also given in the infinitive.

If there is a vowel change in the *du* and *er/sie/es/man* forms in the present tense, this is shown under **3rd person present**. The vowel change is the same for the *du* form. In some verb tables the changed vowel is highlighted. If there is no vowel change, this column may often be left blank.

The *er/sie/es/man* form of the **imperfect** is given. This is identical to the *ich* form. The other forms of the imperfect can be worked out from it.

The **past participle** column reveals not only the form of the past participle (needed to form the perfect and other compound tenses), but also whether a verb takes *sein* or *haben*. A very common abbreviation for this is an * for verbs which take *sein*. In some verb tables, if it is possible for a verb which usually takes *sein* to take *haben* in some circumstances, then the asterisk may be in brackets. The rules are given in '*Haben or sein?*' on page 29. If in doubt, assume such verbs take *sein* – it is much more frequent. Verbs which take *sein* in the perfect and other compound tenses do not have either an accusative object or a passive.

The perfect tense

The perfect is the most frequent past tense used in speech and informal writing such as letters, to talk about actions which are over. It is formed in two parts, with the present tense of *haben* or *sein* and, at the end of the clause or sentence, the past participle of the verb in question. The present tense of *haben* or *sein* is referred to as the auxiliary verb. Perhaps the German term *Hilfsverben* is clearer!

Weak verbs

The vast majority of weak verbs, including reflexives, form the perfect tense using *haben* as the auxiliary (see: '*Haben* or *sein?*' below).

The past participle is usually formed by adding *ge-* to the infinitive, removing the *-en* and replacing it with *-t*, as in **ge**spiel**t**.

If the infinitive ends in *-den, -ten, -chnen, -cknen, -dnen, -fnen, -gnen,* or *-tnen,* then an extra *-e* is added before the final *-t* for pronunciation reasons.

If the infinitive ends in *-ieren,* then no *ge-* is added, as in: *repariert, studiert.*

No *ge-* is added if the verb starts with a prefix which does not separate. These prefixes are: *be-, emp-, ent-, er-, ge-, miß-, ver-* and *zer-.*

Example

erzählt   mißhandelt

If the verb has a prefix which **does** separate, it is tacked onto the past participle ahead of the *ge-,* as in *ab**ge**holt.*

Once the past participle has been formed, the only change in the verb is to the auxiliary.

Example

ich habe ... gespielt	wir haben ... gespielt
du hast ... gespielt	ihr habt ... gespielt
	Sie haben ... gespielt
er/sie/es/man hat ... gespielt	sie haben ... gespielt

Strong verbs

While many of these verbs form the perfect tense with *haben,* a good number of them use *sein* as the auxiliary (see '*Haben* or *sein?*' below).

Because these verbs are irregular, the only safe way to discover the past participle is to look the verb up in a verb table. If the verb you are looking for does not appear to be in the table, consider the possibility that it is a compound of another verb, with one of the prefixes mentioned above at the front. Compounds like *befahren* and *abfahren* behave just the same as *fahren,* for example.

Some dictionaries and glossaries list only the vowel changes. So *fahren* would appear as *fahren (ä, u, a).* The final vowel in the list is the past participle vowel, the other two being the third person singular present and the imperfect (see 'How to read a verb table' on page 28).

The same rules about prefixes which do or do not separate apply as for weak verbs (see above).

Examples

essen

ich habe ... gegessen	wir haben ... gegessen
du hast ... gegessen	ihr habt ... gegessen
	Sie haben ..... gegessen
er/sie/es/man hat ... gegessen	sie haben ..... gegessen

kommen

ich bin ... gekommen	wir sind ... gekommen
du bist ... gekommen	ihr seid ... gekommen
	Sie sind ..... gekommen
er/sie/es/man ist ... gekommen	sie sind ... gekommen

Haben *or* sein?

The choice of *haben* or *sein* as auxiliary can cause some difficulty, as there is no equivalent distinction in English. A simple rule of thumb is: Intransitive verbs of motion, plus *bleiben, sein* and *werden,* require *sein* as an auxiliary.

A more sophisticated version of the same rule of thumb includes a mention of a 'change of state', e.g. *einschlafen, explodieren, schmelzen.*

Active and passive

For each tense, the majority of verbs can be **active** or **passive**.

Verbs are active when the subject of the sentence (e.g. *ich, du, Herr Braun, die Männer*) performs the action of the verb. For example, in the sentence *Ich esse die Banane*, the eating is done by *ich*, so it is an active sentence and the verb is active. This may be regarded as the normal state of affairs.

In a sentence with a passive verb, the subject of the sentence suffers the action of the verb. So the previous example becomes: *Die Banane wird von mir gegessen.* It would be possible to omit *von mir*, thus leaving the identity of who performed the action open to speculation.

The passive is found rather more frequently in German than in English, and needs to be known at A-level and AS-level.

There are two sorts of passive in German, the *werden*-passive and the *sein*-passive.

> **HINT**
> *Verbs which take* sein *in the perfect do not have a passive.*

1   The *werden*-passive is the more common, and expresses a process. The passive of all verbs is formed in the same way, regardless of whether they are strong or weak. The principle is that the appropriate tense of *werden* is used in conjunction with the past participle of the verb in question. The past participle is found at the end of the clause or sentence as usual. We have given examples in the *er/sie/es/man* form, which is probably the most common.

Examples

> **HINT**
> *Note that there is* **no umlaut** *on the auxiliary in the imperfect. The pronunciation is crucial to avoiding confusion.*

Tense	hören (weak)	sehen (strong)
Present	er wird gehört	er wird gesehen
Imperfect	er wurde gehört	er wurde gesehen
Perfect	er ist gehört worden	er ist gesehen worden
Pluperfect	er war gehört worden	er war gesehen worden

2   The *sein*-passive is used to show the state the subject of the verb is in as a result of some previous action. It may be helpful to look upon the past participle as an adjective. It is formed for both weak and strong verbs by using the appropriate tense of the verb *sein* and the past participle of the verb in question. It is most commonly found in present and imperfect tenses.

Examples

Tense	
Present	er/sie/es/man ist verletzt
Imperfect	er/sie/es/man war verletzt

Werden-*passive or* sein-*passive?*
Deciding whether to use the *werden*-passive or the *sein*-passive requires you to determine whether an action (*werden*-passive) or a state (*sein*-passive) is being described. The following pairs of examples may help:

Der Tisch wird abgeräumt	*The table is being cleared (someone is in the process of clearing the table)*
Der Tisch ist abgeräumt	*The table is cleared (because someone has already done it)*
Dresden wurde 1945 zerstört	*Dresden was destroyed in 1945 (the action took place that year)*
Dresden war 1946 zerstört	*Dresden was destroyed in 1946 (the action had taken place at some time beforehand)*

If you really cannot decide between the two sorts of passive, the *werden*-passive is about four times as common as the *sein*-passive.

The agent in the passive – whodunnit?
The passive is often used without specifying who performed the action. However, it may be necessary to express who or what performed the action, translating the English 'by'.

There are two possibilities:

1 *von* + Dative – agent (human or inanimate)

Example
Der Ball wurde von dem Mädchen geschlagen   *The ball was hit by the girl*

2 *durch* + Accusative – means

Example
Er wurde durch lautes Singen geweckt   *He was woken by loud singing*

Tools
To show what tools were used, use *mit* + Dative.

Example
Der Stuhl wurde mit einem Schraubenzieher montiert   *The chair was assembled with a screwdriver*

Conditions

There are three sorts of conditions in German. Each sort has a *wenn*-clause and a consequence clause.

Open conditions
The first sort is really a statement of fact.

The *wenn*-clause has the present tense, the consequence clause has the future or present tense.

Example
Wenn du auf der Autobahn einschläfst, wirst du sterben   *If you go to sleep on the motorway you will die*

Possibilities
The second sort of condition expresses things which might – or might not – happen.

The *wenn*-clause has the *Konjunktiv II* (imperfect subjunctive), the consequence clause has *Konjunktiv II*, often in the *würde*-form (conditional).

It follows this pattern:

Examples
Wenn das Wetter schön wäre, könnten wir nach Bonn fahren   *If the weather was (were) fine we could go to Bonn*
Die Kinder wären froh, wenn die Schule ausfallen würde   *The children would be delighted if school was (were) cancelled*
Wir würden es verstehen, wenn es keine Gehaltserhöhung gäbe   *We would understand if there were (was) no pay rise*
Ich könnte nach Berlin kommen, wenn ich Zeit hätte   *I could come to Berlin if I had time*

Regrets and hypotheses
The pluperfect subjunctive form of *Konjunktiv II* is used to express regrets – things which could have happened in the past, but didn't.

Both the *wenn*-clause and the consequence clause are in the pluperfect subjunctive, *Konjunktiv II*.

> **HINT**
> *Avoid using two* würde-*forms in the same sentence where possible.*

Example

Ich hätte es verstanden, wenn es keine Gehaltserhöhung gegeben hätte   *I would have understood if there had been no pay rise*

Wir wären in die Alpen gefahren, wenn das Wetter schön gewesen wäre   *We would have gone to the Alps if the weather had been good*

Modal verbs can be combined with *Konjunktiv II* as follows:

Example

Wir hätten kommen können, wenn wir nicht etwas anderes hätten machen müssen   *We could have been able to come if we had not had to do something else*

Subjunctive

The subjunctive (*Konjunktiv*) has no direct equivalent in English. It is used in set circumstances (such as expressing some conditions), and it is probably best to learn what 'triggers it off'. For a full treatment of what is a complex topic, consult the *Longman A-level Study Guide German*.

1 **After *als ob*, or *wie wenn***, the subjunctive is used as in the following examples:

Er tat, als ob er Bond nicht sähe   *He acted as if he didn't see Bond*
Er tat, als ob er Bond nicht gesehen hätte   *He acted as if he hadn't seen Bond*
Er tat, als ob er Bond nicht sehen würde   *He acted as if he wouldn't see Bond*
Es sieht aus, als ob es schneien würde   *It looks as though it will snow*

2 **Softening the tone** of a request can be done as in the following idiomatic examples:

Ich hätte eine Frage noch   *I have another question*
Das wär's   *That's all*

3 **Reported speech** uses the subjunctive in different ways in the colloquial and formal written registers (a fact which is not always fully understood by Germans). The subjunctive tense used in the formal register is often that used by the original speaker. The following examples may help:

Tense	Original statement	Colloquial register	Formal register	Meaning
Present	Ich esse eine Banane	Sie sagte, sie äße eine Banane	Sie sagte, sie esse eine Banane	*She said she was eating a banana*
Future	Ich werde eine Banane essen	Sie sagte, sie würde eine Banane essen	Sie sagte, sie werde eine Banane essen	*She said she would eat a banana*
Imperfect	Ich aß eine Banane	Sie sagte, sie hätte eine Banane gegessen	Sie sagte, sie habe eine Banane gegessen	*She said she had eaten a banana*
Perfect	Ich habe eine Banane gegessen	Sie sagte, sie hätte eine Banane gegessen	Sie sagte, sie habe eine Banane gegessen	*She said she had eaten a banana*
Pluperfect	Ich hatte eine Banane gegessen	Sie sagte, sie hätte eine Banane gegessen	Sie sagte, sie habe eine Banane gegessen	*She said she had eaten a banana*

HINT ▶ *The subjunctive may be used to distance writers such as journalists from the views expressed.*

▶ *The appearance of the subjunctive can be sufficient to announce that a sentence is reported speech. It may be that there is no equivalent of the* Sie sagte *found in the examples above.*

▶ *When translating from English, beware of being misled by the tense of English reported speech.* **Always** *write down what you think the original speaker said and work from that.*

part II

Summaries of the main methods of assessment with practice questions

1 **Listening**

REVISION TIPS

▶ If you think about it, apart from speaking, listening is one of the most natural language activities. Whenever you come into contact with speakers of the foreign language you will do some listening.

Most learners of German will at first complain that native speakers speak far too quickly. However, this is just a matter of practice. At the end of your A-level course you should be able to understand most speakers on a range of topics. What is often a problem at the beginning is that you can't process the information given quickly enough. With practice this will improve.

Another problem is that some students get used to the voice of their teacher speaking German and can follow him or her but have difficulties with others. Here it is important to make use of all opportunities available to listen to a variety of speakers.

▶ In the examination, you will meet a variety of listening texts. The first part will consist of short items, such as advertisements, newsflashes or weather forecasts. In the second part you will hear longer extracts of interviews or panel discussions. Many exam boards require candidates to use a personal stereo to play the tape. This means that you can work through the tape at your own pace, playing extracts as often as you need to. The disadvantage is that you need to leave enough time to do all the questions, and you need to be able to find places on the tape quickly. A machine with a counter is most suitable.

▶ Other exam boards play a tape to the whole group of candidates. Most extracts will be played through **twice** only. Be aware that the tape cannot be stopped during the examination unless there is a real emergency, so inform the invigilator right at the beginning of the exam if you can't hear properly. Next, make sure that you read the questions carefully. Usually, you will answer in German, but there may also be questions in English and some non-verbal responses such as ticking boxes, true and false, etc. When the tape is playing, concentrate on what you are about to hear. Don't think back over previous questions and don't attempt to read ahead. Work in step with the tape.

▶ Usually, you are **not** allowed to use a dictionary while the tape is playing, which is meant to prevent you from missing information or disturbing others. You are, however, allowed to make notes. When you do, jot down what you hear in German, don't attempt to translate it straight away, as you may lose useful time when doing so. It is a good idea to have a pencil and rubber for notes and a pen or biro for the actual answers. When taking down numbers, remember that Germans reverse units and tens (e.g. *fünfundzwanzig* = literally five and twenty), so when writing it down, write the unit first then add the tens on the left.

▶ In your answers, be relevant. There is no need to repeat the question as part of your answer. The number of marks indicated in the margin will give you a clear idea of how much information you need to give: one mark equals one point for answers written in English; for answers written in German, an extra mark for each question will be given for correct German. The questions are in the order in which the answers occur in the text. So the first question refers to the beginning of the passage, etc. Your answers will be assessed on their communication content and also their linguistic competence. Pay attention to grammar and spelling, so that your German is not ambiguous. If you are not sure of an answer, don't leave a blank but make a reasonable guess based on your overall understanding of the passage. At the end of the examination you will be given time to check your answers. Use this opportunity and for each of your responses ask yourself if they make sense and if what you wrote is actually reasonable.

PRACTICE QUESTIONS

Question 1

Ein Gespräch über Transportprobleme in den Großstädten
Beantworten Sie die folgenden Fragen auf deutsch.

(a) Herr Gyllenhammars Meinung nach, warum muß man das Auto aus den Innenstädten verbannen?
....
....
....[*3*]

(b) Warum wundert sich die Frau über diese Meinung?
....
....
....[*2*]

(c) Wie erklärt Herr Gyllenhammar seine Ansicht?
....
....
....[*5*]

(d) Um Herr Gyllenhammars Pläne zu erfüllen, was wird zuerst vor allem gebraucht?
....
....
....[*3*]

(e) Wie muß die U-Bahn verbessert werden? Geben Sie drei Beispiele.
....
....
....[*4*]
UCLES

Question 2

Erfolgreiche Bewerbung
Im Hörtext zum Thema 'Erfolgreiche Bewerbung' müssen Sie ein Wort suchen, das im Textzusammenhang den folgenden Umschreibungen entspricht. Tragen Sie jeweils das im Text erwähnte Wort neben die entsprechende Umschreibung ein.

(a) Leute, die sich beruflich mit einer Sache befassen ....
(b) hilfreiche Hinweise ....
(c) positive Eigenschaften eines Menschen ....
(d) etwas, das ausgelassen ist ....
(e) persönliche Daten und bisherige Ausbildung ....
(f) Anfang der beruflichen Laufbahn ....
(g) was man verdient ....
(h) etwas unterlassen ....
(i) aufmerksam sein, wenn andere sprechen ....
(j) Arbeit, die man vor einer Unternehmung erledigt ....

[*10*]
London

Question 3
Sie hören jetzt ein Gespräch mit einer Autorin. Beantworten Sie auf deutsch die folgenden Fragen.

(a) Wo arbeitet Charlotte Link?
....[2]

(b) Wie lange arbeitet sie am Tag?
....[3]

(c) Wie kam sie zum Schreiben?
....[2]

(d) Warum fiel es ihr leicht, die Figur von Oliver Cromwell zu recherchieren?
....[2]

(e) Was passierte, nachdem sie das Manuskript an einen Verlag geschickt hatte?
....[2]

(f) Was gab sie nach den ersten Erfolgen auf?
....[2]

(g) Warum ist Geld wichtig für Charlotte Link?
....[1]

NICCEA

Question 4
Sie hören zwei Meldungen aus den Nachrichten. Beantworten Sie die Fragen auf deutsch.

(a) Mehr Frauen an Bord

(i) Was hofft Hans Rudolf Boehmer zu erreichen?
....
....[2]

(ii) Wie viele Frauen sind in der Bundeswehr?
....
....[2]

(iii) Welche Posten haben diese Frauen?
....
....[2]

(iv) Aus welchen Teilen Deutschlands kommen die meisten Bewerber für die Marine?
....
....[2]

(b) Ein klares 'Ja' zu Deutschland

(i) Warum mußte der Aufdruck 'Deutsche Bundespost' von den Briefmarken verschwinden?
....
....[2]

(ii) Warum sprach die Justizministerin gegen den Aufdruck 'Deutschland'?
....
....[2]

(iii) Welches Argument wurde für das Wort 'Deutschland' benutzt?
....
....[2]

(iv) Welches Versprechen gab Bundeskanzler Kohl dem Postminister?
....
....[2]

Question 5
Männergewalt – 'Motivierte Täter'
Elvira Buchwald, 50, Leiterin des Amtes für Gleichstellung in Berlin-Mitte, über ihre Pläne für das erste deutsche Männerhaus.
Beantworten Sie die Fragen auf deutsch.

(a) Für welche Männer ist das 'Männerhaus' gedacht?

....
....[2]

(b) Warum hält Frau Buchwald so ein Haus für sinnvoll?

....
....[2]

(c) Was sollen die Männer im Männerhaus lernen?

....
....[2]

(d) Welche Hindernisse stehen noch vor der Verwirklichung des Projektes 'Männerhaus'?

....
....[2]

(e) Welche Rolle soll der Boxer Henry Maske im Zusammenhang mit dem 'Männerhaus' spielen?

....
....[2]

Question 6
Feldzug der Moralisten
Ein Gespräch zweier Journalisten über die Deutschen und ihre Einstellung zum Leben und zu sich selbst.
Answer the following questions in English.

(a) Summarise the issues which concern many Germans.

....
....[3]

(b) In what way do Germans feel disadvantaged?

....
....[1]

(c) Why do so many find it hard to enjoy their lives?

....
....[1]

(d) Name some things the Germans do for the good of others.

....
....[4]

(e) What is the attitude to the armament industry?

....
....[3]

(f) How does the last speaker sum up the Germans?

....
....[3]

Question 7
Athleten sind pfiffig

Ein Interview mit Wilhelm Schänzer über neue Doping-Kontrollen im Sport.
Beantworten Sie die Fragen auf deutsch.

(a) Wie erfolgreich war Wilhelm Schänzer mit der Doping-Kontrolle?

....
....[2]

(b) Wie unterscheiden sich die neuen Methoden von den alten?

....
....[3]

(c) Welches Beispiel nennt Schänzer für den Erfolg der neuen Methoden?

....
....[3]

(d) Ist Doping nur ein Problem des Spitzensportes?

....
....[2]

(e) Welche anderen Substanzen nennt Schänzer und was sind ihre Wirkungen?
Füllen Sie die Tabelle aus:

Substanz	Wirkung
....	....
....	....
....	....
....	....
....	....

[5]

Question 8
Cool im Osten

Die Jugendlichen in Ost und West werden sich immer ähnlicher. Ausstehen
können Sie sich deshalb noch lange nicht. Ein Interview mit dem Jugendforscher
Hurrelmann.

Beantworten Sie die Fragen auf deutsch.

(a) Was denken ost- und westdeutsche Jugendliche voneinander?

Ossis über Wessis	Wessis über die aus dem Osten
....	....
....	....
....	....
....	....
....	....

[7]

(b) Was haben die Jugendlichen gemeinsam?

....
....[4]

(c) Warum gibt es so wenige Möglichkeiten der Begegnung für Jugendliche?

....

....[3]

(d) Wie verhielten sich Ossis und Wessis beim Kreuzberger Theaterprojekt?

....

....[5]

2 Speaking

▶ The Speaking test, sometimes called the oral examination, is a good chance of showing how well you have mastered German. Many candidates are worried about performing in front of a visiting examiner. However, there is no need to feel over-anxious. All examiners want to see their candidates succeed and they will do everything possible to make students feel relaxed and at ease. In most cases, candidates will meet the examiner informally before the examination so that they can get used to the way the examiner speaks and know who they will meet in the examination.

▶ Much of the examination depends on your confidence. Try to speak fluently and without hesitation. As long as you can keep going and are able to express yourself clearly in German you will do well. Avoid brief answers and clichés or stereotypes. If you make sweeping statements such as *Die Rolle der Frau in Österreich ist Kinder, Kirche, Küche* or *Deutschland nach der Wende hat viele Probleme* you can be sure that the examiner will ask further questions in order to find out what you mean. It is useful then to have some phrases with which to introduce your opinion, but don't forget to have something meaningful to say.

▶ Success in the Speaking test depends largely on the extent of your active vocabulary. The more words and phrases you know the more topics you will be able to discuss. A good preparation for this is active participation in target language discussions in class. The student who sits back in class and prefers to listen will not do too well in the examination situation. So train yourself to be an active contributor.

▶ Don't worry too much about the grammatical accuracy of your statements. Of course, you will need to know the essential points of German grammar (it sounds bad if you don't remember to use *sein* with common verbs like *gehen, fahren, bleiben* in the perfect) but smaller points may not stick out so much and will not distract from a good impression. Remember, at A-level your range of language needs to be wider and more complex than at GCSE. Don't limit yourself to simple main clauses but make use of subordinate clauses to express reasons, or give sequences of time. If in the heat of the moment you forget to place the verb at the end of a subordinate clause, don't worry – many Germans make that mistake as well. If you notice you have made an error or if you get muddled in a sentence you can always stop and rephrase what you have said.

▶ One of the nice things about the Speaking test is that you can be in control. You can steer the direction of the discussion or conversation by asking questions yourself. The examiner will usually only give short answers (after all, you are meant to be speaking), but you can then use the response to strengthen your own argument.

▶ In the Speaking test, depending on the examination board you take, you will face a variety of tasks. There can be role-play and general conversation, discussion of a visual stimulus, discussion of a topic chosen by the candidate and a presentation. The role-play and general conversation may sound familiar from GCSE, but don't be misled. At A-level a much higher standard is required. The role-plays are far more open-ended and not closely scripted, so that you have to respond spontaneously. Also, the general conversation will not be a sequence of simple questions about yourself. It may cover current issues, such as unemployment, drugs, the environment, German unification, etc. You are not expected to have any detailed knowledge about any of these topics but should be able to discuss the issues at the level of intelligent dinner party conversation. You may also be asked about your future plans and you will need to explain your decisions.

▶ When you come to discuss the visual stimulus you will usually be asked comprehension-type questions and will then talk about the issues arising from the stimulus. You will get 15–20 minutes to study this material (which could be a short article, an advertisement, a collection of pictures and headlines or some statistical information which is presented in the form of a graph or diagram) and to think of possible matters arising. During this preparation try to think of vocabulary which you will need, try to anticipate possible questions and make a brief summary of the stimulus material. Make sure you refer back to the material when appropriate and use the language given in it.

▶ Most examination boards will ask you to prepare a topic either for a presentation or a discussion. When choosing your topic, make sure it is relevant to a German-speaking country. Often examination boards specify a list of topic areas from which you must choose, e.g. the environment, the education system, youth, etc. When preparing for your presentation and discussion of your topic begin by making sure you have a good grasp of the relevant vocabulary. Then think of the main points which you want to raise. Don't become too obsessed with figures, statistics and dates but concentrate on the issue and its significance. Be able to explain why you have made your choice and why it is important.

Don't over-rehearse your presentation, and resist the temptation of learning it by heart. However, it is a good idea to record yourself and listen to it. Make sure that you sound interesting and gain the examiner's attention. It is a good idea to gather some visual illustrations of what you are presenting, but when you do this make sure they are relevant and that you actually refer to them. There is no point in bringing pictures in just for the sake of it. They must enhance what you are trying to say.

Finally, try to imagine the sort of questions the examiner may ask about your presentation. Work with a friend, your teacher or language assistant to give you practice runs at presenting your topic and answering questions. Remember that you are not allowed to bring a full script into the examination but only a card with a few headings or key words to act as a memory aid.

Some useful phrases for presenting arguments and opinions:

Meinungen	Opinions
Ich bin der Meinung, daß	*I am of the opinion that*
Ich bin der Ansicht, daß	*I am of the opinion that*
Ich glaube, daß	*I think / believe that*
Ich meine, daß	*I think that*
Ich denke, daß	*I think that*
Ich finde, daß	*I find that*
Für mich ist wichtig, daß	*For me it is important that*
Für meine Begriffe ist...nötig	*In my opinion...is necessary*
Wichtig wäre für mich, daß	*It would be important to me that*
Wie ich das sehe,	*As I see it*
Man darf...nicht vergessen	*One must not forget...*
Man muß auch...bedenken	*One must also consider...*
Meiner Meinung nach braucht man	*In my opinion one needs*
Es geht uns alle an, daß	*It is a matter of concern to all of us that*
Im allgemeinen	*In general*
Es ist aber auch eine Frage von	*It is also a question of*
Ich würde aber raten, daß	*I would advise*
Soweit das mich angeht	*As far as I am concerned*
Dagegen ist einfach nichts zu sagen	*One cannot say anything against it*
Ich finde, das Problem ist auf... zurückzuführen	*I think the problem can be traced back to...*

Zustimmen	Agreeing
Da gebe ich Ihnen recht	*I agree with you*
Sie haben recht	*You are right*
Das stimmt	*That's correct*
Ich bin ganz Ihrer Meinung	*I agree with you completely*
Ohne Zweifel	*Without doubt*
Ich bin damit einverstanden	*I agree with that*
Das finde ich auch	*I think so, too*

Ablehnen	Refusing/disagreeing
Ich muß Ihnen aber widersprechen	*I must contradict you*
Leider kann ich nicht zustimmen	*Unfortunately, I cannot agree*
Ich bin ganz anderer Meinung	*I have a quite different opinion*
Andererseits muß man auch sagen, daß	*On the other hand one must also say that*
Ich bin nicht damit einverstanden	*I do not agree with that*
Das kann ich nicht akzeptieren	*I cannot accept that*
Das mag sein, aber	*That may be, but*
Trotzdem wäre es möglich, daß	*Nevertheless, it would be possible for*
Aber gleich wichtig für mich wäre	*Equally important for me would be*
Zweifellos stimmt es oft, daß...,aber	*Undoubtedly it is often true that...but*
Das stimmt gar nicht, ganz im Gegenteil	*That is not true, quite the opposite*
Es hat doch keinen Sinn,	*There is no point in*
Nein, das sehe ich nicht ein, daß	*No, I don't see why*
Ich finde, das liegt eher daran, daß	*I think it is caused more by*
Das finde ich nicht von Bedeutung	*I do not consider that of importance*

Gegenargumente	Counter-arguments
Das kann man aber nicht beweisen	*One cannot prove that*
Das ist aber nicht bewiesen	*It is not proven*
Das ist schon möglich, aber	*That may be possible, but*
Ist es wirklich so, daß	*Is it really true that*
Ich frage mich, ob	*I wonder whether / if*
Das würden die meisten Leute nicht gern akzeptieren	*Most people would not be willing to accept that*
Sie dürfen nicht hinnehmen, daß	*You must not simply accept the fact that*
Das Schwierige an so einem Plan könnte sein, daß	*The difficulty with such a plan could be that*
Sie dürfen nicht vergessen, daß	*You must not forget that*
Das ist nicht zu leugnen, aber	*That cannot be denied, but*

Vorschläge	Suggestions
Ich schlage vor, daß wir	*I suggest that we*
Ich würde vorschlagen, daß	*I would suggest that*
Mein Vorschlag wäre, ...zu machen	*My suggestion would be to*
Ich möchte dazu sagen, daß	*I would like to add that*
Meiner Meinung nach sollte man zuerst...	*In my opinion one should first*

Erklären	Explaining
Sehen Sie nicht ein, daß	*Don't you see that*
Aber verstehen Sie nicht, daß	*Don't you understand that*

Wie erklärt man diesen Trend?	*How does one explain this trend?*
Ob es daran liegt, daß	*Whether it is it because of*
Ob es möglich ist zu sagen,	*Whether it is possible to say*
Vor allem finde ich, liegt es an	*Most of all I think it is caused by*
Ohne...wäre die Situation nicht so schlimm/hoffnungslos	*Without...the situation would not be so bad/hopeless*
Den Einfluß von...darf man nicht vergessen	*One must not forget the influence of...*
Wenn Leute ein Bedürfnis nach... haben, ist es vielleicht auf... zurückzuführen	*If people have a need for...it can perhaps be traced back to...*

Zugeständnisse machen / Making concessions

Ich wollte das nicht ganz glauben	*I did not really want to believe that*
Ich war einfach anderer Meinung, aber	*My opinion was different, but*
Das stimmt genau	*That is exactly right*

Andere herausfordern / Challenging others

Finden Sie nicht, daß	*Don't you think that*
Was sagen Sie dazu?	*What do you say about it?*
Im Gegensatz zu	*In contrast to*
Im Gegenteil!	*On the contrary!*

Abwägen / Weighing up

Einerseits...andererseits	*On the one hand...on the other hand*
Auf der einen Seite, auf der anderen Seite	*On the one hand...on the other hand*
Wenn man...richtig bedenkt, muß man sich fragen,	*If one really considers..., one must ask oneself*
Die Vorteile davon sind..., die Nachteile aber	*The advantages of it are..., the disadvantages however*
Für die meisten Leute aber ist es keine Frage von	*For most people it is not a question of*
jedoch	*however*
trotzdem	*in spite of this*
immerhin/nichtsdestoweniger	*nevertheless*
Man darf nicht vergessen, daß	*One must not forget that*
Man muß bedenken/beachten, daß	*One ought to consider that*
Dabei ist zu bedenken, daß	*One needs to think about*
Wir sollten auch...in Erwägung ziehen	*We also need to take...into account*
im Grunde genommen/grundsätzlich	*basically*
in erster Linie/vor allem	*above all*
nicht nur...sondern auch	*not only...but also*
sowohl...als auch	*both...and*
...sowie auch	*...as well as*
statt...zu	*instead of...*
Statt immer nur zu klagen, kann man auch etwas Konstruktives tun	*Instead of just complaining one can also do something constructive*
anstatt, daß	*instead of*
im übrigen/noch dazu	*over and above that*
außerdem/darüber hinaus	*anyway/in addition*

Einleiten	Introducing
Es geht um	*We are concerned with*
Es handelt sich um	*It is a matter of*
Es handelt von	*It deals with*
Es ist eine Frage von	*It is a question of*
Es betrifft uns alle, daß	*It concerns us all that*
Es geht uns alle an, daß	*It concerns us all that*
Es ist Geschmacksache, ob	*It is a matter of taste whether*
Es ist eine umstrittene Frage	*It is a matter of controversy*
Es besteht die Möglichkeit, daß	*There is the possibility that*
Eine entscheidende Rolle spielt hier	*A decisive part is played by*
Von Bedeutung ist hier auch	*Also of importance here is*
Viele weisen auf die Wichtigkeit von... hin	*Many point to the importance of...*

Zusammenfassen	Summing up
Im Endeffekt	*In the end*
Letzten Endes	*In the end / Finally*
Entscheidend für mich ist, daß	*For me it is crucial that*
Es ist nicht zu zweifeln, daß	*It is not to be doubted that*
Es ist nicht zu leugnen, daß	*It cannot be denied that*
Es läßt sich nicht widerlegen	*It cannot be refuted*
Es liegt auf der Hand, daß	*It is obvious that*
offensichtlich	*obviously*
selbstverständlich	*of course*
Auffallend ist dabei, daß	*It is striking that*
Aus diesem Grund ist zu schließen, daß	*For this reason one must conclude that*
Daher / Daraus ist zu schließen	*From this it is to be concluded*
Schließlich / zum Schluß	*Finally*
Alles in allem	*All in all*
Um alle Punkte zusammenzufassen	*to sum up*
Um nach...zu beurteilen	*In order to judge according to*

Zeitenfolge	Sequence of time
im Laufe der nächsten Jahre	*in the course of the next few years*
in den letzten Jahren	*in recent years*
in letzter Zeit	*recently*
in nächster Zeit	*in the near future*
gegenwärtig	*at present*
fortan / von jetzt an	*from now on*
über viele Jahre hinaus	*over many years to come*

Begründen	Giving reasons
aufgrund dessen	*because of which*
unter diesen Umständen	*under these circumstances*
Der Grund besteht darin, daß	*The reason for it is that*
Anlaß dazu gibt	*The reason for it is*
Was dazu geführt hat, ist, daß	*What has led up to this is that*
Ausgangspunkt von...war	*The starting point for this was*
Das ist oft auf...zurückzuführen	*This can often be traced back to*
Das liegt daran, daß	*It is because*
Entscheidend ist, ob / daß	*The crux of the matter is whether / that*
Es nützt nichts, daß jetzt alle protestieren	*It is no good everyone protesting now*

Das hat als Folge, daß	The consequence of it is that
Folge davon ist, daß	The upshot of it is that
Daraus ergibt sich, daß	It follows that
Das Ergebnis davon kann nur...sein	The result of it can only be
Die Situation spitzt sich zu	The situation is becoming more acute
Hat sich die Lage verbessert?	Has the situation improved?
Ich will nicht bestreiten, daß..., aber was hilft es, wenn	I do not want to question the fact that..., but what good is it if

Vergleichen	**Comparing**
einigermaßen	to some extent
es sei denn	unless
in großem Maße	to a great extent
nicht im geringsten	not in the slightest
lange nicht/keineswegs	not at all/not really
in dieser Hinsicht	in this respect
in vieler/aller Hinsicht	in many/all respects
im Vergleich mit	compared to
im Verhältnis mit	in relation to
mit Ausnahme von	with the exception of
von...abgesehen	apart from

PRACTICE QUESTIONS

Question 1

Sehen Sie sich die verschiedenen Tabellen zur Arbeitslosigkeit in Deutschland an.

BRUTTOLOHN eines Durchschnittsverdieners
jährlich in Mark, ab 1991 Gesamtdeutschland

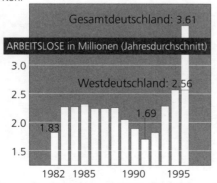

Ernüchternde Bilanz
Die wirtschaftliche Entwicklung unter der Regierung Kohl

Resignation in Deutschland
Arbeitslosenquoten im Vergleich (Jahresendwerte)

Source: Der Spiegel, April 1996. Reproduced with courtesy of SpiegelVerlag

(a) Sind die hohen Löhne schuld an der hohen Arbeitslosigkeit?

(b) Was sind die Probleme der Arbeitslosen?

(c) Was könnte die Regierung machen, damit mehr Arbeitsplätze geschaffen werden?

Question 2
Rollenspiel
Nach Ihren A-levels wollen Sie ein Jahr als Au-pair in der Schweiz verbringen. Sie sprechen am Telefon mit dem Personalleiter einer Agentur. In Ihrem Gespräch müssen Sie die folgenden Punkte klären:

► Warum Sie in der Schweiz arbeiten wollen
► Welche Erfahrungen Sie mit Kindern haben
► Welche Aufgaben ein Au-pair hat
► Ob die Möglichkeit eines Sprachkurses besteht
► Wie hoch das Taschengeld ist
► Ob die Reisekosten gezahlt werden
► Wieviel Urlaub es gibt
► Sie wünschen sich eine Familie in einer mittelgroßen Stadt

3 Reading and writing

REVISION TIPS

Reading is an important part of your examination. Usually 20 per cent of your final grade depends on the result of your Reading paper, but you also need to read German questions in the Listening test and there will be German stimuli in the Writing examination and the Speaking test. So, reading will really constitute a good third of your A-level examination.

Be active

Reading gives you a good chance to increase your range of vocabulary. Try to use the words and phrases you read in your own speaking and writing.

When tackling a reading text don't be put off if you don't understand every word. Read it through attentively and try to get the overall point which is made. After a first reading you should have an idea what the text is about. Then, start with a more detailed understanding, looking up words you don't know in a dictionary (see 'Dictionary work' on page 4). When doing this, remember that in German many words are made up of various components. There are compound nouns, for example *Versicherungsgesellschaft*. You will find *Versicherung* and *Gesellschaft* in your dictionary. Put the two meanings together and you will get 'insurance company'.

Prefixes

Prefixes change the meaning of a word, so knowing their common meanings helps.

Noun prefixes
Erz-	arch, thoroughgoing (e.g. *Erzbischof* archbishop)
Ge-	(a) added to a root word to show repeated or long-running activity (b) added to show a collective sense (e.g. Gebusch *clump of bushes*)
Fehl-	mistaken (e.g. Fehlentscheidung *wrong decision*)
Grund-	basic, fundamental, essential (e.g. Grundschule *primary school*)
Haupt-	main (e.g. Hauptstraße *main street*)
Miß-	to show an opposite or negative (e.g. Mißtrauen *mistrust*)
Mit-	co-, fellow- (e.g. Mitschüler *fellow pupil*)
Nicht-	non (e.g. Nichtraucher *non-smoker*)
Riesen-	enormous (e.g. Riesenrad *big wheel* (at a fairground))
Rück-	backwards (e.g. Rückfahrkarte *return ticket*)
Un-	opposite, unusual (e.g. Unglück *bad luck* (opposite of luck))
Ur-	original, great- (as in generations) (e.g. Urgroßvater *great-grandfather*)

Verbs with separable prefixes
ab-	normally means away, down, off (e.g. abfahren *to depart*, abschneiden *to cut off*)
an-	usually conveys the idea of approach or start of an action (e.g. anfahren *to set a vehicle in motion*)
auf-	up or on (e.g. aufsteigen *to mount* (horse, bike))

aus-	out (e.g. ausgehen *to go out*)
ein-	to get used to something (e.g. eintragen *to wear in* (shoes, clothes)) also the notion of 'into' (e.g. einfuhren *introduce*)
los-	usually refers to the start of something (e.g. losgehen *to set off*)
mit-	conveys cooperation, accompanying (e.g. mitkommen *to come with someone*)
nach-	to follow (e.g. nachlaufen *to run after*)
vor-	either to do something in advance or to demonstrate something (e.g. vorzeigen *to demonstrate* (to show something in front of someone))
weg-	away (e.g. wegfahren *to go away* (on holiday))
weiter-	gives the idea of continuing an activity (e.g. weiterlesen *to continue reading*)
zurück-	to return or back (e.g. zurückgeben *to give back*)

Verbs with inseparable prefixes

be-	used to indicate providing something with something else (e.g. (sich) behelfen *to make do*)
ent-	either escaping or going away or removing something (e.g. entkommen *to escape*)
er-	expresses a change of state or great thoroughness (e.g. erleben *to experience* (to live through something))
ver-	(a) finishing, going away (e.g. vertreiben *to expel*)
	(b) wrongly or excessively (e.g. verschreiben *to misspell*)
	(c) to express opposites (e.g. verkaufen *to sell* (opposite of *kaufen*))
zer-	conveys the idea of 'in pieces' (e.g. zerstören *to destroy*)

In formal texts you will often find long, complex sentences. Remember that the verb in subordinate clauses will be at the end, sometimes quite a distance away from its subject. So try to roughly analyse a sentence, dividing it into main and subordinate clause. Identify the subject and the verb which goes with it. Work out the tense of the verb (past, present or future), then look for the object of a clause (to whom something is done, or who receives something). A good active understanding of German grammar will help you with reading tasks. When finishing the process of reading, ask yourself what the main point of a text is. Is there a clear message, does it make sense? If you are not sure, you will need to take another look.

Clichés

Especially in journalistic writing you will come across a number of clichés, which are phrases with often surprisingly simple meanings:

in Anbetracht der Tatsachen   *in view of the circumstances*
in angetrunkenem Zustand   *drunk*
im Anschluß daran   *after that*
der Auftakt zu (+ Dat.)   *the signal for*
die Frage aufwerfen   *to raise the question*
sich übereinstimmend aussprechen für (+ Acc.)   *to vote unanimously for*
auf die lange Bank schieben   *to put off*
Bedenken hegen   *to harbour doubts*
Begleiterscheinungen   *side-effects*
in groben Zügen darstellen   *to outline in broad terms*
die derzeitige Lage   *the current situation*
sich distanzieren von (+ Dat.)   *to dissociate oneself from*
eine Einigung erzielen   *to reach an agreement*
einen Gesetzentwurf einbringen   *to introduce a bill (to parliament)*

ein Gesetz verabschieden   *to pass an act of parliament*
von einer erheblichen Größenordnung   *big*
jüngsten Nachrichten zufolge   *according to latest reports*
es kam zu einer Kundgebung   *there was a demonstration*
es kam zu Auseinandersetzungen mit der Polizei   *there was fighting with the police*
die Männer wurden handgreiflich   *there was hand-to-hand fighting*
die Lage hat sich entspannt   *the situation has calmed down*
die Lage hat sich verschärft   *the situation has become tense*
in zunehmendem Maße   *increasingly*
Maßnahmen zur Sanierung der Wirtschaft   *measures to improve the economy*
der (heftige) Meinungsaustausch   *a (heated) exchange of words*
in Mitleidenschaft ziehen   *to affect*
mitunter   *including*
der mutmaßliche Täter   *the probable culprit*
der angeblich Verantwortliche   *the alleged culprit*
der Plan scheiterte   *the plan failed*
ein heiß umstrittener Punkt   *a hotly disputed point*
die Möglichkeiten sondieren   *to sound out the possibilities*
die Stellungnahme   *statement, opinion*
Stellung nehmen zu (+ Dat.)   *to comment on*
der Tatort   *the scene of the crime*
die Übergangsregelung   *temporary measure*
die Meinungsumfrage   *opinion poll*

Alternatives to the verb sagen

Ein Sprecher   meinte
gab zu verstehen
erklärte
betonte
behauptete
verkündete
wies daraufhin
beteuerte
versicherte

Advice on comprehension questions

Make your answers relevant. There is no need to begin by rephrasing the question. If there are four marks for a question, you can be sure that your answer will need to contain four points. Comprehension questions are nearly always set in the order in which the answers occur in the text. So the answer to the last question will probably not be in the first paragraph.

PRACTICE QUESTIONS

Question 1

"Große Schrumpfen"

Interview mit dem Berliner Berufsforscher Hermann Schmidt

Schmidt, 61, ist seit 1977 Präsident des Bundesinstituts für Berufsbildung in Berlin.

SPIEGEL: Woche für Woche gehen Tausende von Arbeitsplätzen verloren. Welche Jobs haben in Deutschland noch Zukunft?

Schmidt: Die meisten neuen Stellen werden im Dienstleistungssektor entstehen. Im Jahr 2010 arbeiten nur noch 30 Prozent der Beschäftigten in der Industrieproduktion.

SPIEGEL: Welche Berufsgruppen werden dann besser dastehen?

Schmidt: Die Sicherheits-, Umwelt- und Pflegeberufe werden wichtiger, Freizeit- und Tourismusberufe wachsen. Das stärkste Plus erwarte ich in der Informationsvermittlung – also nicht nur in klassischen Medienberufen, sondern auch bei Unternehmensberatern, Anwälten, Anlage- und Steuerexperten, Wirtschaftsprüfern oder Ausbildern.

SPIEGEL: Wird das den aktuellen Stellenabbau ausgleichen?

Schmidt: Kurzfristig nicht. Langfristig wird der Pflege- und Gesundheitssektor dazu am stärksten beitragen, schon wegen der steigenden Zahl alter Menschen.

SPIEGEL: Bankberufe galten stets als besonders krisensicher, nun baut auch die Finanzbranche Stellen ab. Können Sie die Banklehre noch empfehlen?

Schmidt: Ja, aber nicht, weil bei den Banken viele neue Stellen entstehen. Der Beruf wird anspruchsvoller, immer mehr Bankangestellte haben Kontakt mit Kunden, müssen Informationen aufarbeiten und vermitteln. Was den Menschen in einer Banklehre beigebracht wird, nützt in allen Wirtschaftsberufen.

SPIEGEL: Wer werden die Arbeitgeber der Zukunft sein?

Schmidt: Eher kleine Betriebe. Schon heute schrumpfen vor allem die Großen, bei vielen Kleinen entstehen trotz Krise neue Arbeitsplätze. Besonders gute Aussichten haben Handwerksbetriebe, die als Dienstleiter auftreten. Der Handwerksgeselle der Zukunft wird seine Kunden beraten müssen, er wird eigenständige Aufträge bekommen und an Ort und Stelle die Rechnungen auf einem Laptop schreiben.

SPIEGEL: Worauf müssen sich die Arbeitnehmer noch einstellen?

Schmidt: In Zukunft wird es die lebenslange Arbeit in der gleichen Branche oder gar beim gleichen Arbeitgeber immer weniger geben.

SPIEGEL: Was bedeutet das für Berufseinsteiger?

Schmidt: Eine breite Grundausbildung wird wichtiger. Generalisten haben, bis auf wenige Ausnahmen, bessere Chancen als Spezialisten.

SPIEGEL: Sind die Deutschen auf die Veränderungen am Arbeitsmarkt vorbereitet?

Schmidt: Absolut nicht. Bei der Erstausbildung stehen wir zwar im internationalen Vergleich ganz gut da. Aber bei der Weiterbildung müssen wir noch schwer zulegen.

Lesen Sie den Text 'Großes Schrumpfen' und beantworten Sie die Fragen. Sie müssen **auf deutsch** antworten.

Wählen Sie aus der unten angegebenen Liste zehn Verben aus, um die Textlücken zu ergänzen. Jedes Verb darf nur einmal benutzt werden.

(a) Viele Deutsche .... wöchentlich ihren Job.

(b) Der Produktionsbereich ist am schwersten ....

(c) Herr Schmidt meint, daß unter anderen die Umweltindustrie die besten Berufschancen ....

(d) Unternehmensberater werden zukünftig an Bedeutung ....

(e) Die größere Zahl alter Menschen wird dazu ...., daß immer mehr Leute im Gesundheitssektor .... werden.

(f) Auch in der Finanzbranche .... man Entlassungen zur Zeit, aber Herr Schmidt .... noch eine Banklehre, weil die Ausbildung nützlich für alle Berufsbereiche ist.

(g) Die Bankangestellten .... jetzt viele Aufgaben, die mehr Kontakt mit Kunden ....

> erfordern, wählen, erfüllen, verlieren, gewinnen, betroffen, gefallen, empfiehlt, bietet, beitragen, macht, beschäftigt, erlebt.

AEB

Question 2

FORUM

GESCHICHTEN VON MENSCHEN

Zufall oder Planung?

Eutin am 22. Juni 1955: Der 24jährige Bankangestellte Helmut Schumacher aus Bremen übernachtet während einer Radtour in der Eutiner Jugendherberge. Da trifft eine Klasse dänischer Teenager ein, unter ihnen Ruth Christensen aus Kopenhagen. Zufall oder Planung? Beide sind zum Küchendienst eingeteilt, und bei Helmut fängt es an zu knistern. Mächtig freut er sich, als Ruth nach getaner Arbeit mit ihm durch die Stadt bummelt. Adressen werden ausgetauscht, und nach einigen Wochen werden die Postsäcke zwischen Bremen und Kopenhagen schwerer. Ostern 1956 reist Helmut zu Familie Christensen und läßt sich begutachten. Er übernachtet im Hotel. 'Das wolle ihre Mutter so!' Der jungen Beziehung tat das offenbar gar nicht gut, denn nun folgen drei Jahre Sendepause. Erst auf seinen eindringlichen, schriftlich geäußerten Wunsch 'and don't forget to come to Bremen!' knattert sie im Juli 1959 mit ihrer Vespa in die Hansestadt. 'Da hat's so richtig gefunkt.' Am 25. März 1960 wird geheiratet. Dreißig Jahre nach dem jugendherbergsgemäßen Erst-Flirt startet die ganze Familie zur Erinnerungstour nach Eutin. Das war im Juli 1985. Preisfrage: Wo wird 2000 das 40jährige Ehejubiläum gefeiert werden?

Beantworten Sie die folgenden Fragen **auf deutsch**. In Ihren Antworten dürfen Sie Wörter oder Ausdrücke aus dem Text benutzen, aber das Abschreiben ganzer Sätze oder Abschnitte ist nicht erlaubt.

(a) Wie ist Helmut Schumacher 1955 nach Eutin gefahren?
....[1]

(b) Was haben Ruth und Helmut nach der Arbeit in der Küche gemacht?
....
....[2]

(c) Erklären Sie mit eigenen Worten: '... und nach einigen Wochen werden die Postsäcke zwischen Bremen und Kopenhagen schwerer.'
....
....[3]

(d) Welche Schwierigkeiten hat Helmut in Kopenhagen erlebt?
....
....[3]

(e) Was geschah am 25. März 1960?
....[1]

AEB

Question 3

Leben für den Beruf – oder auch nicht

Das Schicksal des deutschen Mannes ist das Arbeitsleben. Abends kaputt, morgens noch müde und doch grausam frisch rasiert, Zeit für Frau und Familie, nur wenn der Beruf es gerade zuläßt, so verbringt er alle seine Jahre zwischen zwanzig und sechzig. Fast könnte er einem leid tun.

Warum geben sich die Männer also mit diesem Schicksal zufrieden? Die einfache Ungeneigtheit, auf besondere Privilegien zu verzichten, wäre wohl die Antwort des Zynikers. Oder ist es die schlichte Macht der Gewohnheit, oder die Angst, daß das Eingeständnis anderer Interessen als der beruflichen schier unmöglich ist, wenn man Ehrgeiz hat? Und wer hat schon keinen, wenn Aufstieg und Erfolg mit dem Wahn der eignen Wichtigkeit, der Teilnahme an der Macht, und einem Einkommen locken, das man bitter braucht, denn seit der Ankunft der Kinder ist die Frau als Mitverdienerin längst ausgefallen. Allmählich wird der Beruf zu einer Zwangsjacke.

Oder sollte es Männer geben, die anders leben wollen? Man verweist auf eine wachsende Zahl von Belegen dafür, daß es solche Männer gibt, wohl unterstützt von dem Wunsch vieler Frauen, ihr Leben in allen Bereichen mit einem Mann tatsächlich zu teilen, statt ihm nur die unbeliebten Hausarbeiten abzunehmen und dafür auf eigene Berufschancen zu verzichten.

Wissenschaftler haben herausgefunden, daß zehn Prozent aller Männer gerne weniger arbeiten würden, und bei jungen Männern mit guter Ausbildung und jenen Jobs, die angeblich 'den ganzen Mann' verlangen und ihm dafür das Privatleben abschneiden, sind es gar 20 Prozent. Würden diese Männer ihrem Wunsch nachgehen, könnten nicht nur ihre Frauen arbeiten, sondern alle Arbeitslosen der Bundesrepublik. Außerdem finden Männer, die nicht nur für den Beruf leben, selbst diesen Beruf befriedigender als ihre eifrigen Kollegen. Sogar die finanziellen Einbußen drücken sie nicht, weil anderes wichtig ist.

Beantworten Sie die folgenden Fragen in Ihren eigenen Worten auf deutsch:

(a) Warum könnte der deutsche Mann einem leid tun?   [3]

....

....

(b) Warum findet er das hohe Einkommen verlockend?   [3]

....

....

(c) Welche Rolle wollen viele Frauen loswerden?   [3]

....

....

(d) Warum wollen wohl mehr gut ausgebildete junge Männer weniger arbeiten?   [3]

....

....

(e) Inwiefern ändert sich die Einstellung zum Leben von Männern, die weniger
    arbeiten?   [3]

....

....

UCLES

Question 4

Lesen Sie den folgenden Text. Füllen Sie die Lücken mit passenden Wörtern aus und beantworten Sie in vollständigen Sätzen die Fragen, die folgen.

Projekt Wandse

Ihrem Motto gemäß, 'global denken – lokal handeln', haben 20 junge Naturschützer in Wandsbeck für einen Teil der Wandse, eines kleinen Fluß, der mitten durch den Hamburger Stadtteil Wandsbeck fließt, die Verantwortung übernommen. Für ihre engagierte ehrenamtliche Arbeit hat die Jugendgruppe 1989 einen mit 10.000 Mark dotierten Preis bekommen.

Wie bei vielen Flüssen wurden in den 60er Jahren auch bei der Wandse die Ufer mit Tropenholz befestigt. Diese sinnlose Maßnahme hatte schlimme Folgen für die Natur. Für viele Vögel gab es keine Nahrung mehr, da Frösche und andere Wasserlebewesen ausstarben. Die Jugendlichen entfernten zuerst das Tropenholz, damit sich die Wandse wieder selbst ihr Flußbett graben konnte und neue Feuchtgebiete entstehen würden.

Eine andere wichtige Arbeit war das Entfernen von ortsfremden Pflanzen, die aus Übersee importiert wurden und hier die einheimische Vegetation verdrängt hatten. Damit niemand die Jugendlichen mit 'Landschafts-Chaoten' verwechselt, wenn sie beispielsweise junge Bäume fällen, verteilen sie vorher an Anwohner Informationsblätter. Regelmäßig werden Presseartikel veröffentlicht, um andere Leute von ihrer Arbeit in Kenntnis zu setzen.

Projekt Sternberger Anger

In vierjähriger Arbeit haben Schüler und Jugendliche in Angermünde mit Unterstützung der Behörden eine etwa drei Hektar große Fläche in ein Naherholungsgebiet mit einem Naturlehrwald umgewandelt. Dieser Naturlehrwald ist für viele Schulklassen und Naturfreunde zum lebendigen Anschauungsobjekt und Ziel von Ausflügen geworden. Schule in frischer Waldluft statt im staubigen Klassenzimmer – so macht auch der Biologieunterricht Spaß. Das ganze Gelände wurde in verschiedene Abteilungen mit unterschiedlichen Schwerpunkten eingeteilt. Es gibt ein Bildungs- und Informationszentrum, ein Wetterhäuschen mit Instrumenten zur Wetterbeobachtung und einen rekultivierten Teich. Die Bestimmung von Pflanzen, Bäumen und Tieren steht auch auf dem Programm. Ein massiver Beobachtungsstand, der einer ganzen Schulklasse Platz bietet, lädt zur Beobachtung von Vögeln und Waldtieren ein. Ein Platz mit Grill- und Feuerstelle wird auch von den Jugendlichen und Erwachsenen gern benutzt. Dieser Naturlehrwald ist inzwischen weit über Angermünde hinaus bekannt und wurde unter Naturschutz gestellt.

(a) Füllen Sie die Lücken aus. Sie haben die folgenden Wörter zur Auswahl:

> erzählt, zerstört, Essen, verschönert, Futter, Vegetation, Pflanzen, ausstarben, freiwillige, ausgestorben, eigenwillige, informiert

(i) Eine Gruppe von 20 jungen Naturschützern hat für ihre
.... Arbeit einen Preis erhalten. [1]

(ii) Die Ufer der Wandse waren in den 60er Jahren ....
worden. [1]

(iii) Vögel hatten kein ...., weil Frösche und andere
Wasserlebewesen ausstarben. [1]

(iv) Unter anderem haben die jungen Leute .... entfernt.
[1]

(v) Sie haben die Anwohner durch Informationsblätter und Presseartikel über
ihre Arbeit .... [1]

(b) Beantworten Sie diese Fragen.

    (i) Wie lange hat man gebraucht, um dieses Projekt zu realisieren?

....[1]

    (ii) Warum macht jetzt der Biologieunterricht Spaß?

....[1]

    (iii) Was gibt es zur Wetterbeobachtung?

....[1]

    (iv) Von wo aus kann man hier Vögel und Waldtiere beobachten?

....[1]

    (v) Wie weiß man, daß dieser Naturlehrwald inzwischen bekannt geworden ist?

....[1]

NICCEA

Question 5
Lesen Sie den folgenden Text:

Nur wer die Menschen liebt, kann so viel Elend verkraften

Ulli ist erst 28, aber man könnte ihn glatt für 50 halten. Ihm fehlen drei Zähne, sein Haar ist strähnig, der Parka hat wohl noch nie eine Reinigung gesehen. Seit zwei Jahren hat er keine Wohnung und keine Arbeit mehr. Sein Zuhause ist stundenweise ein Raum am Südausgang des Frankfurter Hauptbahnhofs. Ulli ist Stammgast in der Bahnhofsmission, dem einzigen Ort, an dem er nicht auf Ablehnung stößt und schon mal ein liebes Wort hört. 'Eine gute Einrichtung', sagt er und mümmelt an seinem Margarinenbrot. 'Um zehn müssen wir allerdings weg. Da kennen die kein Erbarmen.'

Die, das sind die 16 hauptamtlich und 30 ehrenamtlich tätigen Helfer der Frankfurter Bahnhofsmission, die im Schichtdienst rund um die Uhr arbeiten. 365 Tage im Jahr, egal ob Weihnachten, Ostern oder Silvester. 200 000 Menschen wurde im letzten Jahr geholfen. Die Stadt Frankfurt bezuschußt zwar die Mission, aber in erster Linie ist sie auf private Spenden angewiesen.

Die Bahnhofsmission wurde Ende vergangenen Jahrhunderts für Frauen vom Lande gegründet, die sich in der Stadt Arbeit suchten. Seit dem 1. April 1989 leitet Antje Spory 'Deutschlands größte Sozialstation'. Sie ist die Frau eines Pfarrers, hat drei erwachsene Kinder und ist seit zehn Jahren dabei.

Tag für Tag werden die Helfer mit viel Elend konfrontiert. Antje Spory sagt: 'Wer die Menschen nicht liebt, kann das nicht verkraften. Aber man darf die Probleme der anderen nicht zu seinen eigenen machen. Man muß auch hart durchgreifen können. Um 22 Uhr ist für die Penner hier Schluß, weil wir schließlich an die Reisenden denken

müssen, die nachts hier Zuflucht suchen. Eine Kneipe soll's nicht sein.' Natürlich berührt es sie, daß sie Obdachlose in die Kälte schicken muß. Oder wenn sie die vielen jungen Drogenabhängigen sieht, die manchmal kaum noch laufen können. 'Man stumpft nicht ab, aber wir können uns nicht nur um die Ausgestoßenen kümmern.'

Die Reisebetreuung ist eigentlich die Hauptaufgabe der Bahnhofsmission. Seit Jahren steht an jedem Werktag im Dienstplan: 'Umsteigehilfe Herr Z.' Herr Zimmermann ist blind, arbeitet als Telefonist bei der Sparkasse. Wenn ihn die freundlichen Helfer nicht vom Vorortzug abholen und zwei Etagen tiefer zur S-Bahn bringen würden, wäre er verloren.

Ein anderer Fall: Charlotte Greiner. Sie hat Krebs und reist öfter über Frankfurt. Dort hat sie Aufenthalt und muß umsteigen. Sie ruft dann vorher bei der Bahnhofsmission an, wird abgeholt, bekommt einen Kaffee und wird pünktlich zum Anschlußzug gebracht. 'So fühle ich mich sicher', sagt sie.

Vor allem ältere Menschen finden sich auf dem großen Bahnhof nicht zurecht. Sie verirren sich in dem Labyrinth oder verfehlen die Leute, die sie abholen wollten. Viele Reisende suchen auch Hilfe, weil sie bestohlen wurden. Dann muß entschieden werden, ob man das Fahrgeld vorstreckt. Im letzten Jahr kam das fast 5000 mal vor. Etwa siebzig Prozent zahlen später alles zurück.

Im Hinterzimmer, das für die Mitarbeiter reserviert ist, gibt es einen Alarmschalter. Wenn jemand randaliert, genügt ein Knopfdruck, und die Bahnpolizei rückt innerhalb von einer Minute an. Doch bisher war das nur in wenigen Fällen nötig.

Beantworten Sie die folgenden Fragen in ihren eigenen Worten:

(a) Warum verbringt Ulli seine Tage in der Bahnhofsmission?

....

....[2]

(b) Geben Sie Einzelheiten über die Dienstzeiten.

....

....[2]

(c) Wie bekommt die Mission Geld für ihre Arbeit?

....

....[2]

(d) Wie entstand die Arbeit der Mission?

....

....[2]

(e) Was sind nach der Meinung von Antje Spory zwei nötige, persönliche
    Eigenschaften eines Helfers?

....

....[2]

(f) Mit der Ausnahme von Reisenden, was für Leute suchen an der Mission
    Zuflucht?

....

....[2]

(g) Warum wäre Herr Zimmermann verloren, wenn ihm die Mitarbeiter nicht helfen
    würden?

....

....[2]

(h) Warum ruft Frau Greiner bei der Bahnhofsmission an?

....

....[2]

(i) Warum brauchen meistens ältere Leute Hilfe?

....

....[2]

(j) Was geschieht, wenn jemand randaliert?

....

....[2]

NICCEA

Question 6

Weit unten – Korruption in Deutschland

Die Justiz will härter gegen bestechliche Beamte vorgehen. Auch wer nur kleine Geschenke annimmt, soll künftig bestraft werden.

Mehr als fünf Monate saß Karl-Heinz K, Geschäftsführer des Polizeiausrüsters SITEC, im Gefängnis von Hannover ein, dann nahm er sich das Leben. Die Firma SITEC war bundesweit als 'Deutschlands erfolgreichstes Unternehmen für Körperschutzausstattungen' (so die Eigenwerbung) im Geschäft. Jahresumsatz des Unternehmens: zweistellige Millionenbeträge.

Doch nicht nur SITEC verdiente gut, sondern auch eine Clique von Polizeibeamten, die Karl-Heinz K mit bis zu sechsstelligen Summen schmierte. Zwei Bestochene kamen in Untersuchungshaft. So habe angeblich ein Beamter, beim Innenministerium in Nordrhein-Westfalen für Polizeiausrüstung zuständig, eine halbe Million Mark von Karl-Heinz K kassiert. Der Schweriner Polizeidirektor, der 70 000 Mark einsteckte, wurde schon im September zu zweieinhalb Jahren Haft verurteilt.

Im Fall SITEC soll es aber nicht nur die Großen treffen. Auch gegen die kleinen Abzocker in den Behörden wird vorgegangen. So ermittelt die Staatsanwaltschaft gegen Beamte, die sich ab und zu von Karl-Heinz K zum Essen in teure Restaurants einladen ließen, oder gegen jene, denen der SITEC Chef zu Weihnachten kleine Präsente zukommen ließ: eine Flasche Obstler für 78 Mark oder ein Körbchen mit Wein und Champagner für 128 Mark.

In allen Bundesländern dürfen Beamte selbst kleinere Geschenke nicht ohne Genehmigung annehmen – so das deutsche Beamtenrecht. Bislang wurden Bagatellverstöße selten geahndet. Im Fall SITEC soll das anders werden. Disziplinarverfahren laufen inzwischen schon gegen viele niedersächsische Polizisten.

Den Staatsanwälten geht es um Abschreckung. Die Justiz ist alarmiert seit immer häufiger in deutschen Amtsstuben korrupte Staatsdiener auffliegen und den Beamtenstand, der Jahrzehntelang als weitgehend unbestechlich galt, in Verruf bringen.

Der Fall SITEC liefert jetzt den Vorwand, gegen schwarze Schafe in den Reihen der Beamten vorzugehen. In Schleswig-Holstein sollen Beamte künftig bereits 20 Mark teure Geschenke anmelden müssen. Erste Erfolge der Staatsanwaltschaft stellen sich schon ein: zuhauf werden jetzt auch kleinere Präsente nachträglich gemeldet – nicht nur solche der Firma SITEC.

(a) Finden Sie die im Text gebrauchten Synonyme für die folgenden Wörter und Wendungen:

(i)	die Haftanstalt	(vi)	Erlaubnis
(ii)	beging Selbstmord	(vii)	kleine Verstöße
(iii)	bestach	(viii)	entdeckt werden
(iv)	in den Ämtern	(ix)	in großen Mengen
(v)	Geschenke	(x)	im Nachhinein

(b) Richtig oder Falsch. Kreuzen Sie an:

		Richtig	*Falsch*
(i)	Karl-Heinz K war ermordet worden.		
(ii)	Karl-Heinz K hatte Polizeibeamte bestochen.		
(iii)	Zwei führende Beamte hatten von Karl-Heinz K viel Geld bekommen.		
(iv)	Beamte, die nur kleine Geschenke annahmen, bleiben straffrei.		
(v)	Es gibt in Deutschland nur wenige korrupte Beamte.		
(vi)	Auch Beträge von 20 Mark müssen von den Empfängern gemeldet werden.		

[6]

Question 7

Horrorvorstellung

'Ich bin völlig unmusikalisch und kann überhaupt nicht singen.' Das behauptet die Wienerin Marina Wandruszka. Bei der Aufführung von 'Romeo und Julia' im Hamburger Thalia Theater, in der sie heute wieder als Lady Montague auftritt, besteht dafür auch kein Bedarf. Doch hat sich die Schauspielerin inzwischen eine zweite, musikalisch infiltrierte Karriere aufgebaut: als Opernregisseurin. Als nächstes inszeniert sie 'Figaros Hochzeit' in Amsterdam für eine Tournee.

Mit neun Jahren war sie ein kleiner Ballettstar. Ihr Traumberuf allerdings war Regisseurin. Doch dann wurde sie erst einmal Schauspielerin, weil 1967 am Wiener Reinhardt-Seminar, wo sie studierte, Mädchen in der Regieklasse noch nicht zugelassen waren. In Hamburg holte sie das Versäumte nach.

Seit 1985 gehört sie zum Thalia-Ensemble und inszenierte mehrere Stücke mit einer Jugendspielgruppe. 'Das Thalia-Theater und ich, wir lieben uns', sagt die temperamentvolle Künstlerin. Deshalb ist sie auch immer gern bereit, für erkrankte Kollegen einzuspringen. 'Ich kann Texte vom Mittag bis zum Abend lernen und mache alles.'

Ihren Beruf würde sie auch für eine Familie nie opfern. 'Vater, Mutter, Kind – eine Horrorvorstellung.' Töchterchen Paolina (2½) jedoch ist durchaus ein Wunschkind. In St. Georg sind die beiden zu Hause. Marina Wandruszka liebt den Stadtteil. Noch lieber allerdings würde sie auf einem Bauernhof in den Bergen leben. 'Mit einem Theater gleich nebenan.'

Beantworten Sie die folgenden Fragen auf deutsch:

(a) Welchen zweiten Beruf hat Marina Wandruszka? [*1*]

....

(b) Warum konnte sie zu Anfang nicht Regisseurin werden? [*1*]

....

(c) Wie zeigt sich ihre Liebe für das Thalia Theater? [*2*]

....

....

(d) Was denkt Marina vom traditionellen Familienleben? [*1*]

....

Füllen Sie die folgende Biographie von Marina Wandruszka auf deutsch aus:

NAME: *Marina Wandruszka*

HERKUNFTSORT:

WOHNORT:

BERUF:

FAMILIE:

1967:

seit 1985:

[*7*]

Question 8

U- und S-Bahn – Hamburgs neuer Drogenplatz

Fahrgäste beschweren sich über die Belästigung

Mit Zivilstreifen und verdeckten Ermittlern versuchen Bahnpolizei und U-Bahn-Streifen, Dealer und Süchtige aus Hamburger U- und S-Bahnhöfen zu vertreiben. Die Kehrseite dieses Konzeptes: In den Bahnen wurde noch nie so viel und so offen gedealt wie jetzt.

Auch Drogenabhängige scheuen sich immer weniger, vor anderen Fahrgästen Rauschgift zu rauchen oder sich eine Spritze zu setzen. Arndt Malyska, Chef der Hamburger U-Bahn-Wache, sagt: 'Der Trend ist eindeutig.'

Joachim Häger, Sprecher der Hamburger Hochbahn, bestätigt: 'Ungeniert machen Dealer ihre Geschäfte. Das ist aber kein Problem der U- oder S-Bahnen. Das ist schließlich nur das Spiegelbild der Gesellschaft.'

Immer mehr Fahrgäste beschweren sich über die offene Drogenszene. Joachim Haack, Sprecher des Grenzschutz- und Bahnpolizeiamtes Hamburg: 'Vor allem ältere Fahrgäste fühlen sich belästigt, sie haben Angst, zum Beispiel wenn jemand mit der Spritze hantiert.'

Als besonders auffällig gelten die S-Bahnstrecke zwischen Altona und Hamburg-Hauptbahnhof sowie die U-Bahnhöfe Sternschanze, Hauptbahnhof Süd und die Station Wartenau. Die meist schwarzafrikanischen Drogenhändler seien nur mit Zivilfahndern zu überführen, so Haack. Die Zahl von 30 Dealern, die in den vergangenen sechs Monaten in Hamburger S-Bahnen gefaßt wurden, kommentiert Haack so: 'Hin und wieder geht uns einer ins Netz.' Dealer erhalten immer Strafanzeige, Süchtige werden oft nur aus Bahnen oder Bahnhöfen verwiesen.

Answer the following questions in English:

(a) Why are more drug addicts now found in the underground trains?   [*1*]

....

(b) Name two things drug addicts now do quite openly in the trains.   [*2*]

....

....

(c) How do the other passengers react to the activities of the drug addicts?   [*1*]

....

(d) What steps have the police taken to combat the problem?   [*1*]

....

(e) What is done with the people whom the police arrest?   [*2*]

....

....

Schreiben Sie auf deutsch einen Aufsatz von etwa 250 Wörtern zum Thema: 'Wie sollte man das Problem des Drogenmißbrauchs bekämpfen?'

Question 9

Lesen Sie den Wetterbericht für die Schweiz und das restliche Europa.

Unverändert sonniges Europa

Von einigen Nebel- oder Hochnebelfeldern sowie Störungen im extremen Norden und Süden abgesehen, bleibt Europa wolkenlos. Ein kompaktes Hochnebelfeld hat sich von der Nordsee nach Süden und Osten ausgedehnt und bedeckt das Küstengebiet von der Normandie bis zum Ostsee-Eingang. Ebenfalls gegen Süden ausgedehnt hat sich eine Störung über Nordskandinavien, vor allem zulasten Norwegens, das größtenteils bedeckt ist, während Südschweden noch meist sonnig ist. Das übrige Europa ist von Westen nach Osten wolken- und nebelfrei. Auch die Schweiz ist in allen Teilen sonnig, jedoch dunstig, wie die schwach erkennbaren Seen zeigen. Im östlichen Mittelmeerraum ist es als Folge der ortsfesten Störung über dem Südbalkan unterschiedlich bewölkt. Betroffen ist Süditalien mit zum Teil aufgelockerter Bewölkung von Sizilien bis Rom und bis nach Ostsardinien. Von einer atlantischen Störung haben diffuse Wolken Irland überquert und steuern auf Grossbritannien zu.

Berichte und Prognosen

Weiterhin schönes Wetter

Allgemeine Lage. Das umfangreiche Hoch, das von Osteuropa bis zur Nordsee reicht, bestimmt das Wetter in der ganzen Schweiz.

Prognosen bis Mittwoch abend. Weiterhin schönes Wetter. Im Mittelland am Morgen einige Nebelfelder. Temperaturen in den Niederungen am Morgen früh um 2 Grad, am Nachmittag um 19 Grad. Nullgradgrenze um 2700 Meter.

Aussichten bis Sonntag. Im Norden am Donnerstag noch recht sonnig. Am Freitag Übergang zu starker Bewölkung und dann zeitweise Regen; Schneefallgrenze zwischen 700 und 1200 Metern. Im Süden meist sonnig, am Freitag vorübergehend bewölkt. Tendenz für das Wochenende: Im Norden veränderlich, den Alpen entlang meist stark bewölkt und zeitweise Regen; Schneefallgrenze um 1000 Meter. Im Süden mit Nordwind recht sonnig.

Füllen Sie auf deutsch die Tabelle aus:

Gebiet	Wetter	
Nordeuropa, Skandinavien, Ostsee		[2]
Mitteleuropa		[2]
Östliches Mittelmeer		[1]
Südeuropa		[1]
Grossbritannien		[1]

Answer the following questions in English:

(a) What is dominating the weather in Switzerland? [1]

....

(b) What will the weather be like on Wednesday morning? [2]

....

....

(c) Where will you find temperatures below freezing? [1]

....

(d) How is the weather going to change on Friday? [2]

....

....

(e) Will the weekend bring better or worse conditions for skiers? [2]

....

....

4 *Writing*

► Writing at A-level in German is seen by most candidates as the hardest examination task. However, it need not be so. Writing provides you with a good opportunity of showing how well you have mastered the language. When writing, you have time to think about what you are going to say and how you are going to say it, and you can change and improve your work before finally handing it in.

► Make use of the full amount of time given in the examination. There are no prizes for finishing early. Most of the candidates who hand in their work well before the end of the examination will not get the highest marks. On the other hand, don't spend too long on one good answer and then have to rush the rest.

► Remember, good writing implies a good knowledge of vocabulary. Although you may use dictionaries in the examination, it would take too much time to look up all the words you need. Use your dictionary mainly for checking your work and for making sure you have got a few important words right. When learning vocabulary, it is important to include phrases for presenting an argument, drawing up conclusions, etc. (see pages 41–5) In the examination, marks are given for idiom, which means the range of your vocabulary and its 'Germanness', that is phrases and words which are typically German and not translations from English.

► Remember, too, that writing tests your knowledge of grammar. Mistakes which might be overlooked in Speaking will be very noticeable because they are clearly to be seen on the page. So make sure you know the basics, such as endings for nouns and adjectives, use of cases and the tenses. But you will also need to be familiar with word-order (including subordinate clauses), reported speech (so that you can accurately retell the opinions of others) and the passive. For details on grammar points which often cause trouble, see the grammar section on pages 17–32. A full reference grammar is included in the *Longman A-level Study Guide German*.

► You need to bear in mind that at A-level you are expected to write more complex sentences than at GCSE. Simple sequences of subject, verb, object will not gain high marks. In order to express your thoughts fully, you will need to use subordinate clauses, to show cause and effect, to give reasons and to link events in time.

► No matter what type of writing task you are going to do, allow enough time to check your work.

In the examination

Approaching your work:

► Look carefully at all the questions. Read through them and decide which of the options given you are going to choose. Be sure you fully understand the implications of a question. Don't jump on a task because it seems similar to one you may have done earlier in the course. Each essay question needs a specific answer and not just an overall discussion of a topic. So try to look for what distinguishes the task in front of you from others you have done. It simply won't do to repeat a pre-learnt essay on, for example, the role of women in response to a question which deals with women's issues.

► If you have difficulty deciding on a question, or simply getting started, do a brainstorm and write down all the words you know about a certain topic.

► Make an essay plan. There are basically four types of essay:

  - for and against
  - analysis of key features
  - development of an idea
  - comparison and contrast.

Think which type of essay would best answer the question. Then write down some notes on the introduction, main part and conclusion.

To focus your mind on the task in hand, make your plan and notes in German. Try to think in the foreign language. If you can, you will write far more fluently than if you treat it as one large translation exercise from English into German.

The introduction should be more than a mere repetition of the essay title. You should try to interest the reader in what you are going to say, to show why the issue under consideration is important and how you are going to deal with it.

The main part sets out your arguments. Make sure they are in a logical order, leading smoothly from one point to the next. Remember to use appropriate phrases to link the different ideas. Do not jump backwards and forwards. As most essays are going to be around 300 words long, there should be no need to refer the reader back to what you have said earlier.

The conclusion is meant to be more than a final sentence. It must really arrive at a clear result, giving your opinion and drawing all the arguments of the essay together. If you really feel there cannot be an overall conclusion after considering all the arguments, then explain why and invite the reader to decide for him/herself.

Finally, look back over the introduction. Have you really proceeded in the way you said you would at the beginning?

► Next, write the essay. Try to do it swiftly and most of all keep your thoughts in German. Only look up words when you really need to so you don't waste too much time. Aim to get the task finished.

► At the end, check your work. Go over your draft and attempt to correct all errors. Then make your final neat copy. Be careful not to write a completely new essay, but just change or include something when really necessary. Do not make your draft illegible, just in case you run out of time when making the neat copy. If your final essay ends abruptly before reaching the conclusion, the examiner may refer back to your rough version.

The advice given here refers to all Writing tasks, not just the main essay paper. You will find that most examination boards set combined Reading and Writing papers, where the first two texts are used to check comprehension and the third one is the stimulus for an essay related to the issues raised in the texts. The essay will be relatively short, about 200 words.

When dealing with these stimulus-related essays, you must make sure that you actually refer back to the stimulus, rather than writing a general essay.

In some Writing examinations you will be asked to write a formal letter. This may seem like a familiar task, and many candidates consider it an easy option. Of course, all your GCSE experience of writing formal letters will come in handy, but you must always remember that your work now has to be of A-level standard. The letter will have to show a more sophisticated vocabulary and more complex structures. The themes will be far more advanced than at GCSE, where you mainly wrote about enquiries and simple reservations. At A-level letters deal with complaints, job applications, responses to complaints, etc.

PRACTICE QUESTIONS

Question 1

Sie haben diesen Bericht in der Zeitung gelesen. Schreiben Sie jetzt einen Brief von etwa 200 Wörtern an den Chefredakteur, in dem Sie mögliche Gründe für die zunehmende Gewalttätigkeit in der Gesellschaft angeben und einige Lösungen vorschlagen.

Täter schlagen auf der Straße immer gewalttätiger zu

Bonn. Die Gewaltkriminalität auf den Straßen – Raubüberfälle und grundloses Zusammenschlagen von Passanten – ist seit Jahresbeginn erneut gestiegen.

Selbst eine verhältnismäßig ruhige Stadt wie Bonn meldete voriges Jahr 20 Prozent mehr Fälle Anstieg. Dabei zeichnen sich besorgniserregende Trends ab:

► Die Täter werden jünger. In Frankfurt waren voriges Jahr zwei Drittel der Tatverdächtigen unter 21. Frauen, die am Straßenraub teilnehmen, sind keine Seltenheit mehr.

► Angesichts der Sicherheitsvorkehrungen von Banken und Geschäften weichen Täter zunehmend auf Straßenpassanten aus, und da greifen sie zunehmend die Schwächsten: Alte, Kinder und Behinderte.

► Immer öfter treten gleich mehrere Täter dem Opfer entgegen. Sie greifen häufig zu Messern und Sprühgas, mitunter auch zu Schußwaffen. 'Die Polizei muß die Gewaltkriminalität auf den Straßen zu ihrer Schwerpunktaufgabe machen', meint Eike Bleibtreu, Vorsitzender des Bundes deutscher Kriminalbeamter (BDK) in Bonn. Dabei müsse die Schutzpolizei vorbeugen, die Kripo die Struktur der Cliquen erhellen. 'In der Subkultur ist Gewalt mittlerweile zum Nachweis für Härte und Führungsqualität geworden.' Gewaltanwendung sei bereits eine normale, alltägliche Angelegenheit, meint auch Kriminologe Schneider. 'Mit polizeilichen Mitteln allein ist das Problem nicht zu lösen.' Diverse Gewaltkommissionen haben inzwischen zwar kluge Analysen erarbeitet, aber praktisch kaum Wirkung erzielt. Schneider: 'Elternhaus, Schule, Sport und Politik müssen endlich für ein gewaltfreies Klima sorgen. Im Fernsehen wird Gewalt als Unterhaltungsspektakel vermarktet. Oft sind junge Täter ganz fassungslos, was sie angerichtet haben, wenn echtes Blut geflossen ist.'

(from: *Die Welt*)

NICCEA

Question 2

You are working for the Bank der Wirtschaft in New York. In your branch the only German speaker is Frau Edel, Mr Wenzel's secretary. Despite the German name, Mr Wenzel, the Director, has only a reading knowledge of German. As Frau Edel is on leave, Herr Wenzel gives you the letter printed below, and asks you to draft a suitable response.

He highlights the following points which you **must** include in your letter:

► Thank Herr Feder for his letter.
► We have many years of experience in advising companies trying to locate in the United States.
► The opinions he expresses in his letter are correct.
► A growing number of entrepreneurs are turning to the American market.
► Due to the favourable exchange rate it is possible for German companies to buy US firms at a very reasonable price.

- ▶ Suggest that he should come over to see for himself.
- ▶ We would arrange accommodation for him and establish contacts with local companies.
- ▶ Ask him if he speaks English or if we need to arrange for an interpreter.
- ▶ Further useful information can be obtained from the Office of Economic Development.

(Total length: approx 200 words)

G.E.B international
Postfach 34 23
2000 Hamburg 6

Hamburg, den 13.06.19..

Herrn
H. Wenzel
Bank der Wirtschaft
200 Park Lane
New York 10022
USA

Betreff: Gründung einer Niederlassung in Amerika

Sehr geehrter Herr Wenzel,

unser Herr Reich hat uns empfohlen, daß wir uns mit Ihnen zwecks Gründung einer Niederlassung in den Vereinigten Staaten in Verbindung setzen.

Wir finden, daß unsere Produkte für den amerikanischen Markt aufgrund des an Wert verlierenden Dollars zu teuer werden. Durch die Produktion in Amerika könnten wir neue Märkte erschließen und unsere Ware billiger anbieten. Eine solche Niederlassung dürfte uns vor allem den Zugang zu den lateinamerikanischen Märkten erleichtern.

Weiterhin sind wir der Ansicht, daß uns in Amerika ein großes Reservoir an gelernten und hochqualifizierten Arbeitern zur Verfügung stünde, während die Lohnkosten dort vergleichbar und oft niedriger sind. Es scheinen auch größere unternehmerische Freiheiten zu bestehen, die es ermöglichen, in Zeiten der Rezession den Mitarbeiterstab zu reduzieren.

Ferner legen wir Wert darauf, unsere eigenen Erfahrungen durch den direkten Wettbewerb mit amerikanischen Konkurrenten zu verbessern. Auch möchten wir den ständigen Zugang zu den technologischen Fortschritten der amerikanischen Industrie ausnutzen.

Wir wären Ihnen äußerst dankbar für Ihre Stellungnahme und Beratung.

Mit den besten Empfehlungen

G.E.B international

S. Feder
Außenhandel

Question 3

You spent your summer holidays working in a hotel in Switzerland. As your stay progressed you were unhappy about a number of things and on your return to England you decide to write to the hotel to raise these issues with them, not so much expecting any compensation for yourself but rather hoping that other students will fare better.

In your letter include:

▶ the dates between which you worked at the hotel
▶ a brief description of your tasks
▶ the wages paid were lower than expected
▶ your working hours were long
▶ not enough time for your own sight-seeing
▶ unfriendly treatment by senior staff which upset you
▶ hope that other student-workers will be treated better.

Question 4

Schreiben Sie einen Aufsatz von etwa 250 Wörtern:

Entweder
„Ist Rauchen heute noch zu verantworten?'
Oder
„Sollte Zigarettenwerbung ganz verboten werden?'

Question 1
Ein Gespräch über Transportprobleme in den Großstädten

Transcript

Female	*Herr Gyllenhammar, was ist Ihre Meinung zu dem zunehmenden Verkehr in unseren Städten?*
Gyllenhammar	*Fast in allen Metropolen droht inzwischen das totale Verkehrschaos.*
Female	*Wie sollten die Städte darauf reagieren?*
Gyllenhammar	*Wir müssen das gesamte städtische Verkehrssystem noch einmal neu überdenken. Die Innenstadt von München ist in zehn Jahren noch so groß wie heute, die City von Paris oder London ebenfalls. Also können wir in diesen begrenzten Raum nicht immer mehr Autos hineinlassen. Schon in naher Zukunft wird es nur eine Lösung geben. Wir müssen das Auto aus den Innenstädten verbannen.*
Female	*Es überrascht, eine solche Forderung vom Chef eines Automobilkonzerns zu hören.*
Gyllenhammar	*Es mag Sie überraschen. Aber Verkehrsstaus oder ein Chaos auf den Straßen sind doch die schlimmsten Feinde des Automobils. Wenn das Auto nicht mehr den Komfort bringt, den die Leute an ihm lieben, wenn sie mit dem Auto kaum vorwärts kommen, dann verlieren sie den Spaß an ihm.*
Female	*Wie sollen die Leute in die Büros, zu den Geschäften in den Innenstädten kommen, wenn die Autos aus ihnen verbannt sind?*
Gyllenhammar	*Moment. Ein Fahrverbot für Privatautos ist nicht der erste Schritt. Wir brauchen riesige Investitionen in das öffentliche Verkehrssystem. Investitionen in einer Größenordnung, vergleichbar jenen, als das Schienennetz der Eisenbahn gebaut wurde. Wir brauchen eine neue Art öffentlichen Transports, der den Leuten soviel Annehmlichkeiten bietet wie die Fahrt im Privatauto.*
Female	*Wie soll denn die neue Art öffentlichen Verkehrs aussehen?*
Gyllenhammar	*Nehmen Sie die Busse. Wenn sie nur alle 15 Minuten kommen und man an Haltestellen im Freien warten muß, im Winter in der Kälte, in Schnee und Matsch, im Sommer in der Hitze, wenn man im Bus dann wie eine Ölsardine eingequetscht ist, wird man nicht damit fahren wollen. Aber die Busse könnten in den Stoßzeiten alle zwei Minuten kommen. Die Haltestellen können eine Klimaanlage haben. Die Busse selbst müßten bequeme Sitzplätze für alle bieten. Solche Busse gibt es bereits, aber sie werden für Fernreisen eingesetzt.*
Female	*Sollen Busse das Verkehrsmittel der Zukunft sein?*
Gyllenhammar	*Nicht nur Busse. Man wird das U-Bahn-Netz verbessern müssen. Die U-Bahnen müssen sauberer werden, sie müssen häufiger verkehren, und es muß für die Sicherheit der Passagiere gesorgt werden.*
Female	*Herr Gyllenhammar, wir danken Ihnen für dieses Gespräch.*

Answers

(a) Any two of:

Das totale Verkehrschaos droht; in 10 Jahren ist die Innenstadt genauso groß wie heute; man kann in diesen begrenzten Raum nicht immer mehr Autos hineinlassen.

(b) Er ist Chef eines Automobilkonzerns.

(c) Verkehrsstaus/mit dem Auto nicht vorwärts kommen; Chaos auf den Straßen; sind die Feinde des Autos; wenn das Auto nicht mehr den Komfort bringt, verliert man den Spaß an Autos.

(d) (riesige) Investitionen in das öffentliche Verkehrssystem; eine neue Art öffentlichen Transports

(e) sauberer werden; häufiger verkehren; es muß für die Sicherheit (der Passagiere) gesorgt werden

Question 2
Erfolgreiche Bewerbung

Transcript

Bei dieser Bewerbung sollten Sie nichts dem Zufall überlassen. Die Trainings-Videos der FAZ sind von Profis zusammengestellt und geben Ihnen wertvolle Tips. Da ist erstmal die Bewerbung selbst: Wie beschreiben Sie Ihre Stärken? Wie erklären Sie Lücken in Ihrem Lebenslauf? Warum sind Praktika vor dem Berufsbeginn sinnvoll? Wie soll das richtige Foto aussehen? Warum immer eine individuelle Bewerbung? Was sagen Sie zum Thema Gehalt? Und dann die persönliche Vorstellung: Was wird von Ihnen erwartet, und was sollten Sie vermeiden? Wie sollen Sie sich vorbereiten? Wie finden Sie Informationen? Was ziehen Sie an? Welche Fragen werden Ihnen gestellt? Was müssen Sie fragen? Was dürfen Sie nicht fragen? Wann hören Sie besser nur zu? Eine bessere Vorbereitung zum wichtigsten Schritt in Ihrem Leben als unsere Trainings-Videos gibt es nicht!

Answers

(a) Profis

(b) Tips

(c) Stärken

(d) Lücken

(e) Lebenslauf

(f) Berufsbeginn

(g) Gehalt

(h) vermeiden

(i) zuhören

(j) Vorbereitung

Question 3
Interview mit einer Autorin: Hans-Peter Zimmermann spricht mit Charlotte Link, einer deutschen Autorin

Transcript

Frage   *Charlotte Link, wo wohnen Sie?*

Link   *Ich habe eine Eigentumswohnung in München, wo ich auch arbeite.*

Frage   *Und wie sieht's da aus?*

Link   *Total chaotisch. Da lasse ich alles fallen, kann auch niemanden reinlassen.*

Frage   *Wie arbeitet man als Bestsellerin?*

Link   *Von 9 bis mittags. Und dann noch mal von 14 bis 17, 18 Uhr. Die Bürozeiten brauch' ich, sonst bin ich nicht bei der Sache. Mindestens zehn Seiten pro Tag. Handgeschrieben. Die will ich auf jeden Fall geschafft haben.*

Frage   *Wie kamen Sie überhaupt zum Schreiben?*

Link   *Durch Lesen. Ich habe früher alles verschlungen, was mir in die Finger kam. War der Typ 'Unter der Bettdecke schmökern'. Und mit 16, da hab' ich gedacht: Könntest du eigentlich auch mal versuchen. Ich stieß auf die Figur von Oliver Cromwell und habe angefangen zu recherchieren. Das war leicht, denn das Hobby meines Vaters ist Geschichte. Da mußte ich nur in seine Bibliothek gehen und mir alle Bücher über Cromwell heraussuchen. Daraus entstand dann 'Die schöne Helena'.*

Frage   *Ganz schön mutig, sich mit dem Manuskript gleich an einen renommierten Verlag zu wenden.*

Link   *Hätte ich auf andere gehört, wäre nie was daraus geworden. 'Die Verlage schicken die Manuskripte doch sowieso ungelesen zurück', hieß es immer wieder. Aber schon nach zwei Wochen bekam ich Nachricht, wurde nach Hamburg eingeladen.*

Frage	Und?
Link	*Phantastisch. Das war überhaupt ein tolles Jahr. Ich hatte das Abitur hinter mir, einen Studienplatz und jetzt noch das. Wahnsinnig stolz war ich und aufgeregt. Sie sagten, daß sie es drucken wollten. Aber ich müsse noch ein Drittel kürzen. Das war ganz schön hart.*
Frage	*Was passierte mit Ihrem Jurastudium?*
Link	*Das gab ich nach den ersten Erfolgen auf.*
Frage	*Haben längst Ihre erste Million verdient ...*
Link	*Noch nicht ganz. Ich muß zugeben, das Geld bedeutet mir auch einiges. Vor allem Unabhängigkeit.*

Answers

(a) in ihrer Wohnung/zu Hause
(b) von 9 bis mittags; von 14 bis 17/18 Uhr
(c) durch Lesen
(d) Geschichte war Hobby ihres Vaters; hat in seiner Bibliothek Bücher gesucht
(e) nach zwei Wochen hat sie eine Antwort erhalten; wurde nach Hamburg eingeladen
(f) Jurastudium
(g) es bedeutet Unabhängigkeit

Question 4
(a) Mehr Frauen an Bord

Transcript

Marineinspekteur Hans-Rudolf Boehmer möchte mehr Frauen auf seine Schiffe holen. Der Vizeadmiral verweist auf positive Erfahrungen anderer Nato-Länder. Die Bundeswehr hat knapp 2700 Soldatinnen, sie dienen jedoch nur als Sanitäterinnen und in Militärorchestern. Wenn mehr Frauen eingestellt werden, hofft Boehmer, könnte der Mangel an Bewerbern für Unteroffizierposten ausgeglichen werden. Vor allem in Bayern und Baden-Württemberg, wo früher ein Drittel der Seekriegsfahrer rekrutiert wurde, sinken die freiwilligen Meldungen.

Answers

(i) Er will mehr Frauen auf die Schiffe holen.
(ii) Es gibt etwa 2700/etwas weniger als 2700.
(iii) Sie sind Sanitäterinnen oder Musikerinnen (in Militärorchestern).
(iv) Sie kommen aus Bayern und Baden-Württemberg/aus Süddeutschland.

> **Examiner's note** For each question one mark is given for content and one mark for correct German.

(b) Ein klares 'Ja' zu Deutschland

Transcript

Als im Frühjahr der Aufdruck 'Deutsche Bundespost' von den Briefmarken verschwinden mußte, weil die Post privatisiert war, gab es für die Neubenennung zwei Alternativen: 'Deutschland' oder 'Bundesrepublik Deutschland' – ein Problem, das nicht nur Briefmarkensammler umtreibt.

Per Rundbrief ließ Postminister Bötsch zunächst die Ministerpräsidenten aller 16 Bundesländer abstimmen. Ergebnis: ein klares 'Ja' zu 'Deutschland'. Doch Justizministerin Sabine Leutheusser-Schnarrenberger schien das 'Deutschland'-Etikett gefährlich, es fördere 'nationalistische Tendenzen'. Die Angelegenheit mußte ins Kabinett.

Vor den Ministern plädierte Bötsch für das schlichte 'Deutschland'. Den vollen Ländernamen verwendeten eh' nur Liechtenstein oder der Vatikan. Frankreich und Österreich schrieben 'Republik', und den Briten reiche sogar einfach das Konterfei ihrer Queen.

Innen- und Außenministerium stimmten für 'Deutschland'. Der Kanzler, Helmut Kohl, versprach dem Postminister gar, ihn gegen kritische Postbenutzer in Schutz zu nehmen. 'Schieben Sie es einfach auf mich.'

Answers

(i)   Weil die Bundespost privatisiert war.
(ii) Weil es nationalistische Stimmung erzeugen könnte.
(iii) Nur wenige Länder benutzen auf Briefmarken den vollen Ländernamen.
(iv) Wenn es Proteste gibt, will der Bundeskanzler die Verantwortung tragen.

> **Examiner's note** The extracts above are taken from a news bulletin. In each listening examination paper you will find some questions which are based on short broadcasts (news, weather, sports). So it is a good idea to try and listen to the radio and become familiar with that type of listening text.

Question 5
Männergewalt – 'Motivierte Täter'

Transcript

Reporter   *Frau Buchwald, Häuser für mißhandelte Frauen gibt es viele. Sie wollen jetzt ein Haus für prügelnde Männer einrichten. Haben Sie Mitleid mit den Tätern?*

Buchwald   *Nein. Aber ich will Männern, die ihre Frauen schlagen, ein Angebot zur Hilfe machen. Es ist nicht einzusehen, daß immer die Frau als Opfer unfreiwillig die gemeinsame Wohnung verlassen muß und ins Frauenhaus flüchtet. Statt dessen können doch auch die Täter ausziehen.*

Reporter   *Glauben Sie denn tatsächlich, daß solche Männer reumütig in einem Männerhaus Quartier beziehen?*

Buchwald   *Reumütig vielleicht nicht, aber freiwillig. Ich hatte auch schon Anfragen von Frauen und Sozialarbeiterinnen, die Männer soweit gebracht hatten, daß sie bereit waren, die gemeinsame Wohnung zu verlassen. Ein gewisser Druck ist eben manchmal nötig. Es ist auch vorstellbar, daß Männer durch Bewährungsauflagen zum Einzug motiviert werden.*

Reporter   *Zwangsweise soll also niemand eingewiesen werden?*

Buchwald   *Nein, schließlich sollen die Männer in Beratungsgesprächen und Selbsthilfegruppen lernen, die Verantwortung für ihre Taten zu übernehmen und Konflikte gewaltfrei zu lösen. Im Alltag mit anderen können sie dann das friedliche Zusammenleben einüben. Das geht nur mit motivierten Tätern.*

Reporter   *Wann zieht der erste Schläger ein?*

Buchwald   *Wenn die Finanzierung steht. Ein passendes Haus haben wir bereits gefunden. Der Verein 'Mannsarde' wird als Betreiber fungieren. Auch der politische Wille des Senats ist vorhanden. Er muß rund 500 000 Mark pro Jahr bewilligen. Notfalls treiben wir auch mit spektakulären Aktionen Geld für das Projekt auf. Ich will den Boxer Henry Maske für eine Benefizveranstaltung unter dem Motto 'Schlage nur Gleichstarke' gewinnen.*

Answers

(a) Es ist für Männer, die ihre Frauen schlagen.
(b) Weil die Frau als unschuldiges Opfer nicht aus der gemeinsamen Wohnung ausziehen soll./Weil meistens die Frauen die Wohnung verlassen, obwohl sie unschuldig sind.
(c) Sie lernen, ohne Gewalt Konflikte zu lösen, friedlich mit anderen zusammenzuleben.
(d) Die Finanzierung muß noch abgeschlossen werden.
(e) Er soll vielleicht in einer Wohltätigkeitsveranstaltung auftreten.

Question 6
Feldzug der Moralisten

Transcript

Person 1   *Im Jammern und Klagen sind die Deutschen bestimmt Weltmeister. Immer wieder sprechen sie über ihre Sorgen und Nöten.*

Person 2   *Ja. Einmal sind es die Asylanten und die Angst von einer Ausländerflut erdrückt zu werden, dann ist es die Angst vor einer Umweltkatastrophe. Denken wir nur an die Proteste in Gorleben gegen die Atommülltransporte.*

Person 1   *Natürlich. Oder nennen wir auch das Entsetzen über die französischen Atombombenversuche auf dem Mururoa-Atoll.*

Person 2   *Zufriedenheit ist wirklich nicht die Sache der Deutschen. Sie maulen und beschweren sich, daß sie immer zu kurz kommen und von allen übervorteilt werden.*

Person 1   *Dazu kommt, daß sich viele Deutsche noch immer von der nationalen Vergangenheit bedrückt fühlen. Immer wieder glauben sie, daß man ihnen die Judenverfolgung vorwirft.*

Person 2   *Aber auch sonst fühlen sie sich benachteiligt. Man hört Reden wie: Deutsche Autos werden von den Japanern nicht so oft gekauft wie japanische von den Deutschen.*

Person 1   *Wenn dann doch mal ein Funken Lebensglück aufklimmt, hält man gleich inne und fragt: Dürfen wir uns gute Laune leisten, während Millionen in der Dritten Welt verhungern? Oder tragen wir nicht zur Abholzung des Regenwaldes bei, wenn wir einen Hamburger bei McDonald's kaufen? Belastet es nicht die Umwelt, wenn wir täglich frische Wäsche anziehen?*

Person 2   *Ja. Immer hört man im Lande Fragen über Fragen. Man ist problembewußt und durchaus aufgeschlossen. Was fehlt sind wirkliche Antworten. Natürlich gibt es viele gute Menschen, die anderen als Wegweiser dienen wollen.*

Person 1   *Dem stimme ich zu. Die Deutschen haben sich in einen Chor von Gut-Menschen gewandelt, denen es um das Wohl der anderen geht. Man trennt sorgsam den Hausmüll, bestraft Umweltsünder unter den großen Firmen mit Boykott und schickt lastwagenweise Lebensmittel in notleidende Länder. Soll am Deutschen jetzt die Welt genesen, so nach dem Motto: Edel sei der Deutsche, hilfreich und allzeit bestürzt.*

Person 2   *Bestürzt darüber, daß die Welt nicht so ist wie sie sein sollte: friedlich, solidarisch und FCKW-frei.*

Person 1   *Dabei darf man nicht vergessen, daß die Bundesrepublik der zweitgrößte Waffenhändler der Welt ist.*

Person 2   *Aber deutsche Panzer und Raketen sind nicht der einzige Exportartikel 'made in Germany'. Man bemüht sich, Friedenspolitik in alle Welt zu tragen.*

Person 1   *Ist das dann aber nicht doch nur eine Art der Gewissenberuhigung: auf der einen Seite Einkünfte aus Waffenexporten und auf der anderen Seite, der Wille für Weltfrieden zu arbeiten.*

Person 2   *Die Deutschen tun sich schwer mit dem Wohlstand. Sie können und wollen nicht einfach nur genießen und gut leben. Sie fühlen sich für die anderen Menschen verantwortlich.*

Person 1   *Und die Verantwortlichkeit, die man fühlt, wirft eben viele Fragen auf, die dann sich als Klagen und Beschwerden tarnen. Deutsche sind eben Leute mit feinem Gewissen, bewußt ihrer Widersprüche und voller Zweifel.*

Answers

(a) They are worried about the environment, world peace, the problem of poverty in other countries.

(b) They still feel that others blame them for the persecution of the Jews.

(c) They keep thinking about those who are less fortunate.

(d) They are environmentally aware, separate their household waste, give food-aid and boycott firms which pollute the environment.

(e) They have a conscience. On the one hand they like the income from arms' exports, on the other hand they want to work towards world peace.

(f) They are full of contradictions and doubts. They feel their responsibilities and have lots of questions.

Question 7
Athleten sind pfiffig

Transcript

Reporter	*Sie haben im vergangenen Jahr doppelt so viele Doping-Sünder überführt als im Vorjahr. Wird gedopt wie noch nie zuvor?*
Schänzer	*Das glaube ich nicht. Die Steigerung unserer Funde beruht eher auf den neuen Geräten, die bei Tests eingesetzt werden. Wir können jetzt gezielt Spuren verbotener Substanzen herausfiltern.*
Reporter	*Die gedopten Athleten haben also weniger Chancen, unerkannt zu bleiben?*
Schänzer	*Ja. Heute können wir die Einnahme von Anabolika noch feststellen, wenn der Athlet das Präparat schon drei Wochen lang nicht mehr nimmt. Mit Hilfe der neuen Technik ist dies möglich.*
Reporter	*Können Sie dafür ein Beispiel nennen?*
Schänzer	*Ja. Im vergangenen Jahr haben alle über den Anabolika Einsatz bei den als unschlagbar geltenden chinesischen Schwimmerinnen getuschelt. Mit unserem neuen Verfahren haben wir bei den Meisterschaften in Tokio gleich elf Schwimmerinnen überführen können.*
Reporter	*Die Sportverbände reagieren zum Teil mit drastischen Strafen, wie Wettkampfverbot, Ausschluß aus Mannschaften usw. auf Doping-Fälle.*
Schänzer	*Das ist ganz richtig. Dadurch wird eine gewisse Abschreckung erreicht. Aber man muß noch weitergehen. Wir untersuchen ja nur die Spitzensportler. Es besteht die Gefahr, daß im unteren Leistungsbereich, bei Kindern und besonders bei Jugendlichen massenweise gedopt wird.*
Reporter	*Anabolika-Konsum wird oft als Kavaliersdelikt gesehen.*
Schänzer	*Bestimmt. Ich muß aber vor den großen gesundheitlichen Gefahren warnen. Anabolika schädigen Leber und Herz. So kann es zu plötzlichem Tod führen, besonders bei hoher Dosierung.*
Reporter	*Welche anderen Mittel außer Anabolika werden verwendet?*
Schänzer	*Besonders in den USA nehmen Fußballer vor Spielen Kreatinin, das vermehrt Energie gibt. Das Problem mit dieser Substanz ist, daß Kreatinin auch auf natürliche Weise im Fleisch ist. So ist ein Nachweis des Mißbrauchs schwierig. Ebenso nehmen viele Athleten Schmerzmittel vor einem Wettkampf, um sich so über die Schmerzgrenze drücken zu können.*
Reporter	*Worin bestehen denn hier die Gefahren für den Sportler?*
Schänzer	*Durch die Einnahme von Schmerzmitteln vor einem Wettkampf werden Schädigungen von Muskeln und Bändern durch Überbeanspruchung nicht rechtzeitig bemerkt, was zu langfristigen Problemen führen kann.*

Answers

(a) Er hat im vergangenen Jahr doppelt so viele Athleten überführt als zuvor.

(b) Sie können die Einnahme von Anabolika noch nachweisen, selbst wenn der Athlet sie seit drei Wochen nicht mehr nimmt.

(c) Die chinesischen Schwimmerinnen, die mit der neuen Methode überführt wurden.

(d) Nein, auch bei Kindern und Jugendlichen in niedrigen Leistungsklassen wird gedopt.

(e)

Substanz	Wirkung
Kreatinin	vermehrte Energie
Schmerzmittel	höhere Leistung durch Überschreitung der Schmerzgrenze

Question 9
Cool im Osten

Transcript

Reporter   *Wie ist denn das Bild, das ost- und westdeutsche Jugendliche voneinander haben?*

Hurrelmann   *Die Ostler sehen alle Wessis als cool. Sie tragen Markenklamotten und wohnen im Einfamilienhaus. Wessis sind von Natur aus cool, haben alles usw. Die Ossis werden von den Wessis 'Udo' genannt: Unsere doofen Ossis. Man betrachtet sich gegenseitig mit viel Skepsis.*

Reporter   *Gibt es denn keine Gemeinsamkeiten?*

Hurrelmann   *Natürlich gibt es die. Jugendliche aus Ost und West hören die gleiche Musik, interessieren sich für die gleichen Fernsehprogramme. Überhaupt gibt es recht ähnliche Wertevorstellungen. Doch wenn es zu richtigen Begegnungen kommt, so stehen die Vorurteile im Vordergrund.*

Reporter   *Finden Ost und West Jugend nicht zueinander?*

Hurrelmann   *Kaum. Nehmen wir Berlin. Dort bestehen Möglichkeiten zur Begegnung. Aber sie werden nur selten angenommen. Im Schulbereich gilt das Wohnortsprinzip. Man geht eben dort in die Schule, wo man wohnt. Deshalb begegnen sich Ost und West eben nicht im Pausenhof. Die meisten Begegnungen beruhen auf den Bemühungen einzelner Lehrer, Schüler verschiedener Schulen zusammenzubringen.*

Reporter   *Können Sie dafür ein Beispiel nennen?*

Hurrelmann   *Ja. Es gibt zum Beispiel eine Partnerschaft zwischen einer Oberschule im Ostteil der Stadt und einer Gesamtschule im Westteil. Für viele Ostjugendliche ist der Besuch im multikulturellen Kreuzberg ein ganz neuer Eindruck. Zum ersten Mal erleben sie Deutsche, die von früheren Gastarbeitern abstammen.*

Reporter   *Also lassen sich langsam Beziehungen aufbauen?*

Hurrelmann: *Bestimmt. Aber es ist ein langer Weg. Das Zusammenwachsen braucht Zeit. Die Mauer im Kopf besteht noch. Ein Theaterprojektkurs im Kreuzberger Kulturzentrum wäre wegen des gegenseitigen Mißtrauens beinahe geplatzt. Die Ossis hielten die Kreuzberger Kids für Chaoten, während die Westler zunächst die Ossis als Faschisten ansahen. Auch bei der Arbeit am Theaterstück gab es Gegensätze. Die Kreuzberger sprühten vor Ideen, blieben aber nie lange bei der Sache. Die Ossis dagegen arbeiteten konzentrierter, brachten aber zuerst kaum Vorschläge ein. Doch der Zwang zur Zusammenarbeit brachte schließlich Erfolge. Als das Stück aufgeführt wurde, waren alle ganz stolz auf ihr Werk.*

Reporter   *Es bleibt zu hoffen, daß man noch mehr solcher Projekte macht. So läßt sich der Ost–West Gegensatz von der Jugend überwinden.*

Answers

(a)

Ossis über Wessis	Wessis über die aus dem Osten
sie sind cool, haben alles, tragen Markenklammotten, wohnen in einem Einfamilienhaus	Udo: Unsere doofen Ossis

(b) Sie lieben die gleiche Musik, sehen die gleichen Fernsehprogramme, haben dieselben Wertevorstellungen.

(c) Weil man sich in den Schulen nicht begegnet. Man geht immer dort zur Schule, wo man wohnt (Wohnortsprinzip).

(d) Die Ossis machten anfangs kaum Vorschläge, aber arbeiteten konzentrierter; die Wessis waren voller Ideen, aber blieben nicht so lange bei der Sache.

Solutions: Speaking

Question 1

The conversation could go like this:

Examiner	*Unterhalten wir uns jetzt etwas über Arbeitslosigkeit.*
Candidate	*Ja, hier auf dem Schaubildern sieht man, daß Arbeitslosigkeit in Deutschland seit 1982 ständig gestiegen ist. 1991 war die Zahl der Arbeitslosen vorübergehend gefallen, aber vier Jahre später hat sie um fast eine Million zugenommen. Berücksichtigt man die Zahlen für Gesamtdeutschland, so gab es 1995 eine Arbeitslosenrate von 10.9 Prozent.*
Examiner	*Was könnten die Gründe für diese Entwicklung sein?*
Candidate	*Die Löhne sind im gleichen Zeitraum erheblich gestiegen, und zwar um fast 16 000 DM. Es gibt weniger Arbeitsplätze, aber die vorhandene Arbeit wird besser bezahlt.*
Examiner	*Also, wie könnte man diese Situation verbessern?*
Candidate	*Zunächst würde es vielleicht helfen, wenn die Löhne nicht zu hoch wären. Betriebe könnten dann mehr Angestellte und Arbeiter einstellen. Auch sollte der Staat Arbeitsplätze schaffen, besonders für junge Leute.*
Examiner	*Warum gerade für junge Leute?*
Candidate	*Also, ich denke, es ist wichtig, daß junge Menschen eine Chance bekommen, sich einen Beruf zu suchen. Sie bekommen dann die Selbständigkeit, die sie brauchen. Auch wollen sie gerne das anwenden, was in der Schule oder Ausbildung gelehrt wurde.*
Examiner	*Was sind denn die Probleme der Arbeitslosen?*
Candidate	*Ich denke, zunächst einmal fehlt ihnen das Geld. Viele Familien, die keinen Verdiener haben, leiden wirkliche Not. Dann kommen soziale Probleme dazu. Arbeitslose werden oft als minderwertig angesehen. Sie fühlen sich nutzlos. Viele haben sicher auch Langeweile, wenn sie den ganzen Tag zu Hause sind.*
Examiner	*Vielen Dank für dieses Gespräch.*

Examiner's note Note how the candidate refers back to the graphs and statistics provided. Make sure you know how to talk about figures, describe increases, decreases etc. Be prepared to offer explanations where appropriate. Also remember to look at any questions which are provided in the stimulus material. The examiner will usually refer to them at some stage unless you decide to take the conversation in a slightly different direction.

Question 2

Your dialogue could be like this:

Examiner	*Also, warum möchten Sie denn in der Schweiz arbeiten?*
Candidate	*Ich war noch nie in diesem Land, aber ich habe viel über die Schweiz gelesen. Ich bin gern in den Bergen, fahre im Winter Ski und wandere im Sommer. Auch möchte ich ein Land kennenlernen, wo vier verschiedene Sprachen gesprochen werden.*
Examiner	*Das haben Sie sich ja schon gut überlegt. Welche Erfahrungen haben Sie denn mit Kindern?*
Candidate	*Ich habe einen jüngeren Bruder. Er ist erst fünf Jahre alt. Ich passe oft auf ihn auf, wenn meine Eltern ausgehen, und ich spiele oft mit ihm. In der Kirche helfe ich mit beim Kindergottesdienst.*

Examiner	Der kleine Bruder, da haben Sie ja schon eine Vorstellung, wie das ist, mit Kindern zu arbeiten.
Candidate	Ich hätte auch eine Frage an Sie. Was muß ich als Au-pair alles machen, also abgesehen von der Kinderbetreuung?
Examiner	Also, Sie müssen auch im Haushalt helfen. Ein bißchen bügeln vielleicht, oder Geschirr spülen oder auch mal etwas im Garten machen. Das kommt ganz auf die Familie an. Mehr als drei Stunden pro Tag brauchen Sie aber nicht zu arbeiten.
Candidate	Das klingt nicht schlecht. Ich würde auch gerne meine Deutschkenntnisse verbessern. Kann ich einen Sprachkurs besuchen?
Examiner	Ja, dafür bekommen Sie zwei halbe Tage pro Woche frei.
Candidate	Wie sieht es mit der Bezahlung aus? Bekomme ich ein Gehalt oder ist es nur ein Taschengeld?
Examiner	Sie bekommen ein Taschengeld von 75 Franken pro Woche.
Candidate	Wie ich schon gesagt habe, wandere ich gern. Bekomme ich auch Freizeit, so daß ich Ausflüge machen kann?
Examiner	In der Regel haben Sie einen freien Tag pro Woche.
Candidate	Und wie ist es mit dem Urlaub? Wie viele Wochen pro Jahr gibt es?
Examiner	Also, normalerweise gibt es drei Wochen Urlaub. Haben Sie sonst noch Fragen?
Candidate	Ja. Darf man sich aussuchen, wo man arbeiten will?
Examiner	Haben Sie denn da besondere Wünsche?
Candidate	Ja, ich möchte gerne in einer mittelgroßen Stadt wohnen. Großstädte gefallen mir nicht. Da ist es so laut. In einer kleineren Stadt findet man auch leichter Kontakt zu anderen Menschen.
Examiner	Wir werden sehen, was sich machen läßt. Schicken Sie mir so bald wie möglich Ihre schriftliche Bewerbung. Wenn Sie noch andere Fragen haben, rufen Sie ruhig wieder an.
Candidate	Vielen Dank für Ihre Hilfe. Ich habe jetzt eine gute Vorstellung von dem, was mich erwarten kann. Nochmals herzlichen Dank. Auf Wiederhören.
Examiner	Auf Wiederhören.

Examiner's note This candidate does not mention the question about *Reisekosten*. As the overall question does not ask the candidate to include all the points in the list, the student will not lose points for this one omission. However, unless specified otherwise, you should aim to cover as many, if not all, the points mentioned in the question.

3 Solutions: Reading and writing

Question 1

(a) verlieren

(b) betroffen

(c) bietet

(d) gewinnen

(e) beitragen, beschäftigt

(f) erlebt, empfiehlt

(g) erfüllen, erfordern

> **Examiner's note** You will have noticed that there are more verbs given than actually needed to fill all the gaps and also that all the verbs are in their finite form (i.e. with the correct endings). The sentences with the gaps paraphrase the text, but are not direct copies. You will need to look back over the reading passage and find some indication of which verb might suit, e.g. in the text you read: *Woche für Woche gehen Tausende von Arbeitsplätzen verloren.* Sentence (a) of the exercise is a rewording of this. When you look at the list of verbs you will see *verlieren*, which fits in the gap.

Question 2

(a) mit dem Rad/Fahrrad (1)

(b) sie sind in der Stadt – spazierengegangen (1+1)

(c) Helmut und Ruth schrieben sich – regelmäßig/oft (2+1)

(d) er konnte/durfte nicht – bei Ruths Familie – bleiben/übernachten (1+1+1)

(e) sie haben geheiratet/ihre Hochzeit (1)

> **Examiner's note** You can see that in some cases alternatives are given; there may even be more ways of expressing the same idea. The marks at the end of the questions show you how much detail is required. In question (b) there are two marks, therefore you need two pieces of information, i.e. *in der Stadt* and *spazierengehen*.

Question 3

(a) Er lebt nur für seine Arbeit [1]

    Er kommt kaputt nach Hause [1]

    Er hat keine Zeit für die Familie [1]

(b) weil man es braucht [1]

    denn die Frau kann nicht mehr verdienen [1]

    seit die Kinder da sind [1]

(c) ihre Rolle im Haushalt [1]

    wo die Hausarbeiten unbeliebt sind [1]

    und wo sie keine eigenen Berufschancen haben [1]

(d) Der Job verlangt zu viel [1]

    Sie wollen mehr Privatleben [1]

    Sie wollen nicht immer arbeiten [1]

(e) Sie finden den Beruf befriedigender [1]

    Es fehlt ihnen nicht sehr das Geld [1]

    Anderes wird jetzt interessant im Leben [1]

> **Examiner's note** As each question carries three marks, all the answers need three details. In this case the details are not just individual words but ideas or concepts which need to be taken from the text. You cannot simply copy them because each question implicitly asks you also to interpret what you have read. Again, there are

many different ways of expressing the required ideas, and the above answers represent only one of the possible ways of phrasing the replies.

Question 4

(a) (i)   freiwillige
   (ii) zerstört
   (iii) Futter
   (iv) Pflanzen
   (v)   informiert
(b) (i)   vier Jahre
   (ii) weil er jetzt draußen im Wald stattfindet
   (iii) es gibt ein Wetterhäuschen mit Instrumenten
   (iv) man kann sie von einem massiven Beobachtungsstand sehen
   (v)   er wurde unter Naturschutz gestellt

Question 5

(a) Er hat keine Wohnung und keine Arbeit; die Mission ist der einzige Ort, an dem man ihn nicht ablehnt.
(b) Schichtarbeit rund um die Uhr; das ganze Jahr hindurch.
(c) Die Stadt Frankfurt bezuschußt die Mission; hauptsächlich ist sie von privaten Spenden abhängig.
(d) Sie wurde Ende des 19. Jahrhunderts für Frauen vom Lande gegründet, die sich in der Stadt Arbeit suchten.
(e) Man darf nicht zu empfindlich sein; man muß eine starke Persönlichkeit haben.
(f) Obdachlose und Drogenabhängige besuchen die Mission.
(g) Er ist blind; die Helfer müssen ihn vom Vorortszug abholen und zwei Etagen tiefer zur S-Bahn bringen.
(h) Sie hat Krebs; sie reist viel und muß am Frankfurter Bahnhof umsteigen.
(i) Sie verirren sich; sie verfehlen die Leute, die sie abholen wollen.
(j) Sie drücken einen Knopf im Hinterzimmer, und die Bahnpolizei kommt gleich an.

Question 6

(a) (i)   Gefängnis
   (ii) nahm sich das Leben
   (iii) schmierte
   (iv) in den Behörden
   (v)   Präsente
   (vi) Genehmigung
   (vii) Bagatellverstöße
   (viii) auffliegen
   (ix) zuhauf
   (x)   nachträglich

(b) (i)   Falsch
   (ii) Richtig
   (iii) Richtig
   (iv) Falsch
   (v)   Falsch
   (vi) Richtig

Question 7

(a) Sie ist Opernregisseurin.
(b) Weil Mädchen in der Regieklasse nicht zugelassen waren.
(c) Sie übernimmt Rollen für Kollegen, die krank sind.
(d) Es füllt sie mit Horror/ist eine Horrorvorstellung.

Biographie:
NAME:	*Marina Wandruszka*
HERKUNFTSORT:	*Wien*
WOHNORT:	*St. Georg bei Hamburg*
BERUF:	*Schauspielerin und Opernregisseurin*
FAMILIE:	*eine Tochter*
1967:	*Studium am Reinhardt-Seminar*
seit 1985:	*engagiert am Thalia-Theater, Hamburg*

Question 8

(a) Because police and security forces have successfully driven them away from the railway stations.
(b) They smoke drugs; they inject drugs.
(c) They feel frightened.
(d) They have increased the number of plain-clothes officers who travel on the trains.
(e) Dealers are prosecuted; addicts are usually banned from the station or trains.

In the essay, two things are important: First, you need to have a clear structure with beginning/introduction, main part and conclusion; secondly you need to show that your German is of a high standard. This does not just mean spelling, but also grammar and range of language (subordinate clauses, phrases, etc). You are not judged on the merit of your ideas or any factual content.

Sample answer:

Wie sollte man das Problem des Drogenmißbrauchs bekämpfen?

Der Kampf gegen den Drogenmißbrauch muß auf verschiedenen Ebenen geführt werden.

Zum einen sollten Polizei und Grenzschutz gegen Drogenhändler vorgehen. Mit gezielten Aktionen sollten diejenigen, die Drogen anbieten, verfolgt werden. Dazu gehört auch, daß man Informanten den nötigen Schutz gewährt. All zu oft getrauen sich Leute nicht, gegen die mächtigen Drahtzieher des Drogenhandels auszusagen. Ebenso muß der Grenzschutz vermehrt kontrollieren. Obwohl offene Grenzen im Prinzip wünschenswert sind, darf man nicht vergessen, daß Stichproben und Paßkontrollen notwendig sind, um die Bewohner eines Landes vor Drogen zu schützen.

Auf der anderen Seite haben Lehrer, Sozialarbeiter und andere Berufe, die mit Jugendlichen zu tun haben, die wichtige Aufgabe der Drogenaufklärung. Besonders Teenager sind anfällig für Drogen. Deshalb muß in Schulen und Jugendklubs auf die Gefahren der Drogen, die im Umlauf sind, hingewiesen werden. All zu oft wird in der Jugendkultur die Einnahme von Drogen als glamourös und modisch dargestellt. Die harte Realität muß in aller Deutlichkeit gezeigt werden, um Jugendliche vor dem Experiment mit Drogen zu warnen.

Schließlich muß man den schon Drogenabhängigen dringend helfen. Es ist ein Skandal, daß Abhängige oft mehrere Monate auf einen Therapieplatz warten müssen. Den Betroffenen muß die Möglichkeit gegeben werden, aus der Drogenszene auszusteigen. Wenn die Zahl der Konsumenten drastisch sinkt, wird auch der Markt für Drogen kleiner.

Keine der drei Maßnahmen kann alleine das Problem des Drogenmißbrauchs lösen, aber alle zusammen können wesentliche Erfolge erzielen.

Question 9

Gebiet	Wetter
Nordeuropa, Skandinavien, Ostsee	*Nebel, bedeckt*
Mitteleuropa	*wolken- und nebelfrei, sonnig*
Östliches Mittelmeer	*bewölkt*
Südeuropa	*aufgelockerte Bewölkung*
Grossbritannien	*Wolkenbildung*

(a) a high pressure area
(b) early morning mist, temperatures around 2 degrees
(c) in areas above 2700 metres
(d) very cloudy with rain at times
(e) Snowfall is only expected for areas higher than 1000 metres (it was 700 metres earlier on), therefore conditions for skiers will be worse.

Solutions: Writing

Question 1

Your letter will be assessed on three criteria:

► Understanding and response, which means that all required points are included in a clear and coherent manner.

► Selection and presentation, i.e. that the information is well selected and presented in a clear and logical way.

► Use of target language, i.e. you need to show a wide range of vocabulary and high level of accuracy.

Each of these criteria will have equal weight.

Sample answer:

Die Redaktion

In Ihrem Artikel haben Sie ganz richtig betont, daß Straßenkriminalität ständig zunimmt. Man soll nicht weiter hinnehmen, daß besonders Frauen und alte Leute sich kaum noch auf den Straßen sicher fühlen – auch am Tage.

Zur Vermeidung von Überfällen und Angriffen sollte es mehr Polizisten auf den Straßen geben. Die Präsenz des Wachtmeisters erweckt Vertrauen und gibt die Möglichkeit, eventuelle Vorgänge schnell zu melden. Auch hat man mit privaten Sicherungsfirmen, die z.B. Einkaufszentren patrouillieren, gute Erfahrungen gemacht. Ebenso haben sich an vielen Orten Video-Kameras gut bewährt. Sie schützen nicht nur Personen, sondern vermeiden auch unsinnigen Vandalismus.

Jedoch sollten sich die Überlegungen nicht auf den Bereich der Vorbeugung beschränken. Man muß auch die Gründe der Gewalttätigkeit berücksichtigen. Arbeitslosigkeit und Armut müssen gezielter bekämpft werden. Wenn Jugendliche bezahlte Arbeit oder einen Arbeitsplatz haben, eröffnet sich ihnen eine Zukunftsperspektive, und sie werden sich nicht mehr der Kriminalität zuwenden. Nur wenn es gelingt, die Zwei-Klassen-Gesellschaft zu überwinden, wird man auch eine Reduzierung der Straßengewalt sehen. Kurzfristig bedeutet das durchaus eine Steigerung der Staatsausgaben und möglicherweise erhöhte Steuern für besser Verdienende, aber langfristig würde eine bessere Gesellschaft geschaffen werden, und man würde die hohen Kosten für Strafvollzug und Rehabilitation der Kriminellen sparen.

> **Examiner's note** In the above answer, note the use of conjunctions and of phrases for introducing arguments and progression of thoughts. In German letters to the editor there is no need for a greeting (such as 'Dear Sir'), you can come straight to the point, referring back to the article in question.

Question 2

Sample answer:

Sehr geehrter Herr Feder,

wir bedanken uns für Ihren Brief vom 13.06.19..

Die Bank der Wirtschaft hat eine langjährige Erfahrung in der Beratung von Firmen, die sich in den USA ansiedeln wollen.

Wir stimmen Ihrer Analyse der hiesigen Situation voll zu. Jedes Jahr wenden sich neue Unternehmen dem amerikanischen Markt zu. Bedingt durch den günstigen Wechselkurs ist es zur Zeit für deutsche Firmen relativ einfach, amerikanische Unternehmen aufzukaufen.

Am besten wäre es, wenn Sie selbst in die USA kämen, um sich vor Ort von der Lage zu überzeugen. Wir könnten für Sie die nötige Unterkunft buchen und Ihnen auch Kontakte zu einheimischen Firmen verschaffen. Könnten Sie uns bitte auch mitteilen, ob Sie Englisch sprechen oder ob wir für Sie einen Dolmetscher bereitstellen sollten? Weitere nützliche Informationen über eine Geschäftsgründung oder -übernahme erhalten Sie auch vom Office of Economic Development (Büro für wirtschaftliche Entwicklung).

Wir danken Ihnen nochmals für Ihre Anfrage und würden uns freuen, Ihnen weiter behilflich zu sein.

Mit freundlichen Grüßen

Wenzel
Direktor

> **Examiner's note** *The above letter is written in fairly formal language as usually employed in business. You will need to be familiar with this type of German and to know a good number of stock phrases in order to complete the task successfully.*

Question 3

Sample answer:

Sehr geehrter Herr Direktor Meyer,

vom 3. Juli bis 29. August arbeitete ich in Ihrem Hotel zur Sonne. Wie Sie vielleicht noch wissen, bestand meine Arbeit aus einer Mischung aus Küchendienst und Gartenarbeit. Ich mußte Geschirr spülen und mich um den Rasen kümmern.

Als man mir die Ferienarbeit angeboten hatte, war aber von Gartenarbeit nicht die Rede, vielmehr sollte ich am Empfang aushelfen, wo ich meine Fremdsprachenkenntnisse anwenden könnte. Statt dessen mußte ich aber stumpfsinnige körperliche Arbeiten verrichten. Auch gab es bei der Bezahlung Probleme. Statt wie vereinbart 400,– Franken pro Woche bekam ich nur 320,– Franken.

Ich hatte gehofft, in meiner Freizeit etwas von der schönen Landschaft der Schweiz zu sehen, aber leider war meine Arbeitszeit so organisiert, daß ich selten mehr als vier Stunden frei hatte. Es wäre besser, die wöchenliche Arbeitszeit so zu verteilen, daß man zwei Tage pro Woche ganz frei hat, statt mehrere lange Pausen an einem Tag.

Auch müßte man die wöchentliche Arbeitszeit genau festlegen. Ich hatte an eine Vierzigstundenwoche gedacht, in Wirklichkeit aber waren es fast sechzig Stunden.

Was mir den Aufenthalt in Ihrem Hotel aber besonders verdorben hat, war die schlechte Behandlung durch einige der Mitarbeiter. Besonders der Küchenchef und der Hauptgärtner waren sehr unfreundlich und haben meine Arbeit ständig kritisiert. Es schien mir oft, als ob sie mich absichtlich schikanierten.

Ich hoffe, daß mein Brief dazu beiträgt, anderen Studenten ein besseres Arbeitsklima in ihrem Hotel zu verschaffen.

Mit freundlichen Grüßen

> **Examiner's note** *Note that this letter is written in semi-formal language, in contrast to the very formal business letter in question 2. Note, also, the use of the subjunctive, especially for making suggestions.*

Question 4

This is another example of an essay question. The marking will be similar to that for question 1.

This sample essay answers the question '*Ist Rauchen heute noch zu verantworten?*'

Es besteht kein Zweifel, daß Rauchen sehr gravierende Folgen haben kann. Medizinische Forschung hat eindeutig festgestellt, daß Rauchen gesundheitsschädlich ist. Vor kurzem hat selbst ein Zigarettenhersteller die schädlichen Folgen von Nikotin zugegeben.

Keiner, der zur Zigarette greift, kann also sagen, von den gesundheitlichen Folgen nichts gewußt zu haben. Selbst auf den Zigarettenpackungen gibt es deutliche Warnungen. Auch muß man die enormen Kosten für eine medizinische Behandlung von Lungenkrebs, Herz- und Kreislaufschäden ünd anderer Auswirkungen des Rauchens bedenken. Diese Kosten werden von den Krankenkassen übernommen und dann über die Beiträge an die Mitglieder weitergegeben. So zahlen auch Nichtraucher für die durch Rauchen verursachten Krankheiten.

Zieht man alle diese Punkte in Betracht, so muß man die Frage 'Ist Rauchen heute noch zu verantworten?' mit einem klaren 'Nein' beantworten. Auf der anderen Seite sollte man aber auch die Risiken des modernen Lebens bedenken. Unfälle im Straßenverkehr sind ebenfalls für viele Todesfälle und schwere Verletzungen verantwortlich, und trotzdem wird kaum jemand für eine Abschaffung aller Kraftfahrzeuge plädieren. Ebenso schafft die immer weiter steigende Umweltverschmutzung stets neue Schäden für den Körper, denen man sich nur wenig entziehen kann. Daher sagen sich viele, daß. Rauchen nur ein geringes zusätzliches Risiko darstellt, das durch den Genuß des Tabaks mehr als ausgeglichen wird.

Letztlich bleibt es eine Entscheidung des Einzelnen, ob man raucht oder nicht, und jeder muß alle Punkte für sich selbst abwägen.

Timed practice papers

Part 1

Question 1
Füllen Sie diese Tabelle auf deutsch aus:

	in der Nacht	am Tage
Norden	[1]	[2]
Süden	[2]	[2]
Mitte		[2]
Westen		[2]

Question 2
Ergänzen Sie den folgenden Text auf deutsch:

Auf Autobahnen und Landstraßen fließt der Verkehr (a) ....
........................., jedoch befürchtet man auf der A6 wegen (b) ....
.... später am Tag Stauungen. Besonders in den (c) ....
.... müssen Autofahrer mit Behinderungen rechnen. Im
Frankfurter Flughafen gibt es (d) .... wegen
des ungünstigen Wetters in Europa. Reisenden wird empfohlen, sich vor der Fahrt
zum Flughafen nach den Abflugszeiten (e) ....

[5]

Part 2

Question 3

Section A
Kreuzen Sie an, ob die folgenden Aussagen richtig oder falsch sind:

	Richtig	Falsch
(a) Der Hungerstreik im Kali-Bergwerk ist zu Ende.		
(b) Es befindet sich auch eine Frau unter den Hungerstreikenden.		
(c) Für die Arbeiter wird es keine neuen Arbeitsplätze geben.		
(d) Am Freitag fand die Abstimmung über den Streik statt.		
(e) Die Schließung des Bergwerkes ist noch nicht endgültig.		
(f) Die EG-Kommission muß sich einverstanden erklären.		

[6]

Section B
Beantworten Sie die folgenden Fragen auf deutsch:

(a) Aus welcher Zeit weiß Klaus Schucht, was Hungern bedeutet?   [2]
(b) Was dachte er über das Eierwerfen der Demonstranten?   [2]
(c) Wovor hat Klaus Schucht Respekt?   [2]

(d) Welches Ereignis hätte schlimme Folgen für das Verständnis von Ost-und Westdeutschland? [2]

(e) Warum kann die Treuhand ihre Haltung gegenüber dem Bergwerk Bischofferode nicht mehr ändern? [2]

(f) Welchen Vorwurf – laut Herrn Schucht – könnten Westdeutsche der Treuhand machen? [3]

Question 4

Answer the following questions in English:

(a) Describe Herr Patynowski's emotions on his arrest. [3]
(b) What had many people thought about Herr Patynowski? [1]
(c) How does he explain his presence at the scene of the fire? [1]
(d) What alibi does Herr Patynowski have? [2]
(e) How does Herr Patynowski describe the police interrogations? [3]
(f) Why did he not have a solicitor? [1]
(g) What is Herr Patynowski's reaction to the suggestion that he belongs to an extreme right-wing group? [2]

TRANSCRIPTS AND ANSWERS TO PRACTICE PAPER 1

Questions 1 and 2
Sie hören einen Wetterbericht und Verkehrsmeldungen:

Transcript

'Und jetzt die Wettervorhersage für Freitag, den 28. Februar. Zum Monatsende zeigt sich das Wetter sehr unterschiedlich. Beginnen wir im Norden. Nach teilweise heftigen Regenfällen wird es am frühen Morgen zunächst stark bewölkt sein. Später Aufheiterung mit Höchsttemperaturen um 10 Grad. Im Süden Deutschlands, etwa unterhalb der Mainlinie, ist es merklich kälter. Nachtfrost, Glatteis und Nebel machen in der Nacht das Fahren auf Landstraßen und Autobahnen schwer. Während des Tages verschiedentlich Niederschlag, der teils als Schnee, teils als Regen fallen wird. Die Temperaturen steigen von minus 5 Grad in der Nacht bis auf 7 Grad am Nachmittag. Mitteldeutschland bleibt bedeckt mit starken Regenschauern. Temperaturen um 9 Grad.

Nur im äußersten Westen gibt es einen Vorgeschmack auf den Frühling. Dort ist es sonnig und für die Jahreszeit außergewöhnlich mild, bis 14 Grad.

Und jetzt die Verkehrsmeldungen. Auf den Autobahnen und Landstraßen des Landes Hessen liegen keine Störungen vor. Jedoch warnt die Polizei vor möglichen Staus während den Stoßzeiten auf der Autobahn A6, wo es im Bereich des Frankfurter Kreuzes wegen Bauarbeiten zu beidseitigen Sperrungen kommt. Der Flughafen Frankfurt meldet verzögerte An- und Abflüge wegen der ungünstigen Wetterlage in ganz Europa. Reisende werden gebeten, sich vor dem Weg in den Flughafen bei den entsprechenden Gesellschaften nach den Start- und Landezeiten der Flüge zu erkundigen.

Answers to question 1

	in der Nacht	*am Tage*
Norden	*heftiger Regen*	*heiter, 10 Grad*
Süden	*Nachtfrost, Glatteis, Nebel, minus 5 Grad*	*Regen, Schnee, 7 Grad*
Mitte		*Regen, 9 Grad*
Westen		*sonnig, mild, 14 Grad*

Examiner's note You will be expected to include any two of the four answers under Süden – in der Nacht and two of the three answers under Süden – am Tage and Westen – am Tage.

Answers to question 2
(a) ohne Störungen/ohne Probleme
(b) einer Baustelle
(c) Stoßzeiten/Hauptverkehrszeiten
(d) Verzögerungen/Verspätungen
(e) zu erkundigen

Question 3
Hungerstreik zur Sicherung von Arbeitsplätzen

Section A
Transcript
Newsreader:

Der Hungerstreik der mehr als 40 Kumpel im thüringischen Kali-Bergwerk 'Thomas Müntzer' geht weiter. Inzwischen ist auch eine Frau dabei. Kanzler Kohl hat den Beschäftigten in Bischofferode 700 Ersatzarbeitsplätze nach der Grubenschließung angeboten, doch in einer Abstimmung am vergangenen Freitag entschieden sich die Kumpel, den Hungerstreik fortzusetzen. Noch ist allerdings die Übernahme der ostdeutschen Gruben durch die BASF-Tochtergesellschaft Kli und Salz AG, die auch die Schließung der Zeche in Bischofferode vorsieht, noch nicht rechtskräftig: Die EG-Kommission muß zustimmen.

Answers

(a) Falsch	(d) Richtig
(b) Richtig	(e) Richtig
(c) Falsch	(f) Richtig

Section B
Transcript
Interview mit Treuhand-Vorstand Klaus Schucht über Bischofferode.

Interviewer	*Herr Schucht, haben Sie letzter Zeit abgenommen?*
Schucht	*An meiner Figur ist nicht viel dran zum Abnehmen. Ich wiege seit meinem 20. Lebensjahr zwischen 76 und 78 Kilo.*
Interviewer	*Sie wissen also nicht, was Hungern bedeutet?*
Schucht	*Doch. Ich habe zwischen 1945 und 1948 hier in Berlin beinahe Baumrinde gekaut. Als die Kali-Arbeiter aus Bischofferode bei ihrer Demonstration im Mai 3000 Eier gegen die Fassade der Treuhand-Anstalt geschmissen haben, habe ich denen gesagt: Wer noch mit Eiern werfen kann, dem geht es nicht schlecht.*
Interviewer	*Dann kann Sie der Hungerstreik gegen die Schließung der Grube nicht beeindrucken?*
Schucht	*Die setzen für ihre Ziele ihre Gesundheit aufs Spiel. Das macht ja keiner, der sich nur einen Spaß machen will. Davor habe ich Respekt.*
Interviewer	*Was tut die Treuhand, wenn der erste Kali-Bergmann im Hungerstreik stirbt?*
Schucht	*An so etwas wage ich gar nicht zu denken. Das hätte auf das innerdeutsche Verhältnis die schlimmsten Auswirkungen.*
Interviewer	*Würde die Treuhand die umstrittene Fusion der Ost- und West-Kaliwerke dann noch einmal überdenken?*
Schucht	*Das können wir leider nicht, wir haben abgeschlossene Verträge, die von fünf Gremien abgesegnet sind. Das Unvernünftige an dem Hungerstreik ist: Hier gehen die Menschen gegen eine Sache an, die nicht mehr zu ändern ist.*
Interviewer	*Der Hungerstreik zeigt doch, daß es bei den Betriebsstillegungen im Osten nicht mehr um betriebswirtschaftliche Rechnungen geht, sondern um Politik.*
Schucht	*Das stimmt. Dieser Umbruch hier ist fürchterlich, im Grunde genommen ist er unmenschlich. Nach 40 Jahren Stagnation muß abrupt geändert werden, was bei uns im Westen Jahrzehnte Zeit hatte. Aber das Festhalten an alten Strukturen ist noch gefährlicher. Statt 30 oder 40 Milliarden Jahresverlust bei der Treuhand*

kostet es dann das Doppelte. Und die Westdeutschen werden fragen, warum sie das
mit ihren Steuergeldern bezahlen sollen, wo doch im Westen auch Betriebe still-
gelegt werden müssen. Dann haben wir am Ende wieder zwei deutsche Staaten.
Deswegen müssen wir durch diese Sache durch.

Answers
(a) aus den Jahren 1945 bis 1949/aus der Zeit kurz nach dem Krieg
(b) Den Demonstranten geht es noch recht gut, wenn sie Eier werfen können.
(c) Davor, daß Menschen ihre Gesundheit aufs Spiel setzen.
(d) Wenn der erste Bergarbeiter im Hungerstreik stirbt/Wenn der erste
    Hungerstreikende stirbt.
(e) Alle Verträge sind schon abgeschlossen und unterzeichnet.
(f) Daß Ostbetriebe durch Subventionen geholfen wird, während im Westen auch
    Betriebe schließen müssen.

Question 4
Transcript
Nach dem Brandanschlag auf das Asylantenheim in Lübeck wurden fünf junge Männer aus
Ostdeutschland vorübergehend festgenommen. Unser Reporter spricht mit einem der jetzt aus der
Untersuchungshaft Entlassenen.

Reporter	Herr Patynowski, was haben Sie empfunden, als Sie und Ihre beiden Freunde ver-haftet wurden?
Patynowski	Ich war wie vor den Kopf geschlagen, sah mich schon für immer und ewig in einer Zelle sitzen. Manchmal habe ich geheult. Ich war vorher noch nie in meinem Leben in Haft.
Reporter	Für Millionen Bürger galten Sie zwei Tage lang als eine Art Staatsfeind. Für viele galt bereits als ausgemacht, daß Sie und Ihre beiden Freunde das Asylbewerberheim angesteckt haben. Dafür sprach am Anfang auch einiges.
Patynowski	Ich finde das eine Riesenschweinerei. Noch steht ja überhaupt nicht mal fest, ob das Heim überhaupt angezündet worden ist.
Reporter	Sie kamen aus Mecklenburg-Vorpommern. Was hatten Sie mitten in der Nacht in Lübeck zu suchen?
Patynowski	Wir kamen zufällig vorbei, sahen das Feuer, sind in 150 Metern Entfernung aus unserem Auto gestiegen und haben geguckt. Dabei gerieten wir in eine Personenkontrolle der Polizei.
Reporter	Die Beamten haben nicht an Zufall geglaubt.
Patynowski	Ich weiß. Aber wir kamen erst eine halbe Stunde später, als bereits die Sprungkissen aufgeblasen wurden. Zum Glück konnten Zeugen sich erinnern, uns zum Zeitpunkt des Feuerausbruchs an einer 15 Kilometer entfernten Tankstelle gesehen zu haben. Sonst würden wir heute noch sitzen.
Reporter	Wie lang sind Sie vernommen worden, wie viele Beamte waren bei den Verhören dabei?
Patynowski	Insgesamt sieben Stunden, immer von zwei Mann zugleich. Die Polizei war wahnsinnig daran interessiert, uns als Täter zu überführen. Die wollten natürlich Geständnisse.
Reporter	Wurden Sie von den Beamten unter Druck gesetzt?
Patynowski	Nein, die Verhöre waren sehr sachlich, es wurde uns nichts eingeredet. Aber sie ver-suchten, uns immer wieder in Widersprüche zu verwickeln.
Reporter	Warum haben Sie sich keinen Anwalt genommen in einer derart schwierigen Situation?
Patynowski	Das klingt komisch. Ich dachte, ich war's nicht, deshalb brauche ich auch keinen Anwalt.
Reporter	Stimmt es, daß Sie und Ihre Freunde in der fraglichen Nacht eigentlich Autos knacken wollten?
Patynowski	Dazu äußere ich mich nicht.
Reporter	Wann haben Sie von Ihrer Freilassung erfahren?

Patynowski	*Am Freitag morgen um 8.30 Uhr. Da war die Freude riesig groß.*
Reporter	*Und was haben Sie dann getan?*
Patynowski	*Dann haben wir erst mal ein bißchen gefeiert.*
Reporter	*Gehören Sie zur rechtsradikalen Szene in Ihrem Heimatort Grevesmühlen?*
Patynowski	*Nie was damit zu tun gehabt. Ich bin auch kein Ausländerfeind.*
Reporter	*Wirklich nicht?*
Patynowski	*Meinen Sie, die hätten mich sonst rausgelassen? Es besteht kein Tatverdacht mehr. Wir sind eindeutig unschuldig.*

Answers

(a) He was perplexed, he cried, he thought that he would be imprisoned for ever
(b) That he was the arsonist
(c) They were there by chance/they saw the fire and stopped to watch
(d) He was seen at a petrol station 15 km away from the fire at the time when it started.
(e) They were very objective, the police didn't try to talk them into anything, but tried to get them caught up in contradictions
(f) He knew he was innocent
(g) He has never had anything to do with them and is not a xenophobe

PRACTICE PAPER 2 – SPEAKING (APPROX. 15–20 MINUTES)

Question 1

Diskutieren Sie die Vor- und Nachteile des Tourismus.

Question 2

Entspannter können Sie Ihr Ziel kaum erreichen:
Im Audi A4 2.6 und 2.8 spüren Sie den kraft-
vollen Sechszylindermotor – schon bei niedrigen
Drehzahlen. Aber Sie hören ihn nicht.

Audi A4 mit 6 Zylindern.

Audi
Vorsprung durch Technik

(advert reproduced courtesy of Audi)

Verkaufen die Autohersteller Träume oder Realität?

Question 3

Sie machen eine Busreise mit Ihrer Großmutter durch die Schweiz. Der Bus, mit dem Sie von London abgefahren sind, ist vollbesetzt. Das Programm der Reise ist recht voll: Stadtbesichtigungen, Besuche von Kirchen und Schlössern, oft recht lange Fußwege. Jeden Abend sind Sie in einem anderen Hotel. Das Wetter ist zur Zeit sehr heiß. Nach vier Tagen ist Ihre Großmutter sehr erschöpft und möchte nicht mehr weiter. Sie sprechen mit dem deutschen Reiseleiter über Ihr Problem. Sie haben an folgende Möglichkeiten gedacht:

► sofortige Rückkehr nach England
► Aufenthalt im Hotel für die nächsten Tage
► Änderung des Programms.

Mögliche Probleme, die der Reiseleiter nennt:

► Kostenerstattung bei Abbruch der Reise
► Zahlung des Aufenthaltes im Hotel
► wie zurückfahren?
► Wünsche der anderen Reiseteilnehmer.

Verhandeln Sie mit dem Reiseleiter, um das Beste für Ihre Großmutter zu erreichen.

ANSWERS TO PRACTICE PAPER 2

Check with your teacher or consult the syllabus yourself to find out what your oral examination will entail. The papers of the different examining boards vary, so you need to know what you are required to do.

Question 1

There is obviously no telling how the dialogue with the examiner will develop. When you are tackling this kind of 'stimulus' question, it is always good to start with a brief description of what is shown in the picture(s). Then lead on to the more general issue. The aim is to test your knowledge of spoken German, how well and how accurately you can express yourself. Of course, you can use the vocabulary given in the stimulus, but don't limit yourself to it. You are given time before the examination to look at the stimulus and gather your thoughts, but you are not allowed to make notes to use during the actual speaking test.

The following is an example of how the conversation could go.

Examiner	*Wir wollen uns zunächst über Frage 1 unterhalten.*
Candidate	*Ja. Das Bild zeigt eine Reklame für Reisen. Man sieht zwei Touristen am Strand. Sie liegen auf einer Art Boot im Wasser und lassen sich Getränke von einem einheimischen Kellner bringen. Das Wetter ist schön, sonnig. Das alles soll einen Traumurlaub zeigen. In der Ecke oben links sieht man ein startendes Düsenflugzeug. Man sieht viel Rauch, der aus dem Auspuff des Flugzeugs kommt.*
Examiner	*Warum hat man vielleicht die beiden Bilder zusammengebracht?*
Candidate	*Das soll vielleicht zeigen, wie viele Touristen in den Urlaub fahren. Mit dem Flugzeug. Man denkt an die schönen Tage in der Sonne, aber nicht an die Verschmutzung durch das Flugzeug.*
Examiner	*Also sollte man zu Hause bleiben?*
Candidate	*Nein, das glaube ich nicht. Aber Tourismus kann die Umwelt belasten. Nicht nur die Reise mit dem Flugzeug, sondern auch mit dem Auto ist nicht gut für die Umwelt. Auch werden überall große Hotels gebaut. Das ist nicht schön für die Landschaft.*
Examiner	*Sie meinen, Tourismus bringt Nachteile?*
Candidate	*Ja, es gibt Nachteile, so wie zum Beispiel für die Umwelt. Man muß aber auch bedenken, daß es für viele Länder viel Geld gibt. Touristen geben in einem Land Geld aus, das bedeutet Arbeitsplätze usw. für die Leute dort.*
Examiner	*Abgesehen vom Geld, gibt es noch andere Vorteile?*
Candidate	*Für die Touristen selbst ist Reisen gut. Auf dem Bild sieht man, wie sich der Mann und die Frau erholen. Sich erholen ist wichtig. Auch lernt man im Urlaub neue Länder kennen.*
Examiner	*Wenn man am Strand liegt?*
Candidate	*Nein, aber viele Touristen liegen nicht nur in der Sonne, sondern sie gehen auch sich die Sehenswürdigkeiten anzusehen. Man lernt etwas über die Kultur und Geschichte eines Landes.*
Examiner	*Reisen erweitert den Horizont.*
Candidate	*Ja, dem stimme ich zu. Reisen hilft andere Länder zu verstehen. Es kommt aber immer darauf an, was man im Urlaub macht. Ob man Interesse an neuen Dingen hat.*
Examiner	*Das denke ich auch. Es hängt immer vom Einzelnen ab.*

Question 2

Examiner	*Beginnen wir also. Sehen Sie sich Frage 2 an.*
Candidate	*Also auf dem Bild sieht man eine Werbung für ein Auto. Das Auto ist ein Audi A4. Es wird gesagt, daß der Audi gut fährt ohne Lärm. Man hört den Motor nicht, aber spürt die Kraft. Das Bild zeigt das Auto, wie es schnell fährt. Es könnte auf einer Landstraße sein. Der Hintergrund ist verschwommen.*

Examiner	Das ist dann ein Traumauto?
Candidate	Vielleicht. Das kommt auf den Geschmack an. Es ist ein Mittelklassewagen, so wie ihn ein Direktor oder Manager vielleicht hat.
Examiner	Gut. Wie verstehen Sie dann die Frage über Traum und Realität?
Candidate	Ich denke, daß die Wirklichkeit, die Realität oft anders ist. Es gibt viele Staus und man muß langsam fahren. In der Stadt zum Beispiel gibt es viel Verkehr und auch auf der Autobahn. Meistens gibt es viele andere Autos. Man darf und man kann nicht schnell fahren.
Examiner	Warum zeigt man dann nicht in der Werbung, wie es wirklich ist?
Candidate	Ich denke, das würde keine Käufer bringen. Wenn man ein Auto kauft, denkt man nicht an Staus, an den Verkehr, an Unfälle. Man denkt nur an einen bequemen, schnellen Wagen. Der Traum ist, frei zu sein.
Examiner	Was ist denn an einem Auto wichtig?
Candidate	Ich weiß nicht. Ich denke, vielleicht wie schnell es ist, ob es teuer ist. Vielleicht auch der Platz, wenn man Familie hat. Manche Leute wollen auch ein Auto, um damit Freunde und Nachbarn zu beeindrucken. Ein Mercedes vor dem Haus sieht besser aus als ein Mini. Es geht manchmal auch um Sicherheit. Die Kunden wollen Airbag und ABS.
Examiner	Sie haben von der Sicherheit gesprochen. Wie ist es denn mit der Umwelt?
Candidate	Ja, das ist auch sehr wichtig. Das Auto muß sauber sein, einen Katalysator haben. Das ist heute meistens so. Auch kauft man ein Auto, das wenig Benzin verbraucht, denn Benzin ist sehr teuer. Daran denken viele Leute.
Examiner	Das glaube ich auch. Und trotzdem werden in der Reklame solche Bilder gezeigt.
Candidate	Ja, das Auto ist oft mehr als nur ein Verkehrsmittel. Es ist ein Symbol für Freiheit. Man kann fahren, wohin man will. Man ist unabhängig von anderen, zum Beispiel von Bus oder Bahn. Diese Freiheit ist wichtig für viele Menschen, auch wenn man in Realität immer nur den gleichen Weg fährt, von zu Hause zur Arbeit, zum Supermarkt, usw.
Examiner	Danke. Wir wollen jetzt zur nächsten Aufgabe kommen.

Question 3

Examiner	Beginnen wir mit dem Rollenspiel. Ich bin der deutsche Reiseleiter. Guten Tag. Was kann ich für Sie tun?
Candidate	Ich habe ein Problem. Besser gesagt, meine Großmutter hat ein Problem. Sie findet diese Busreise sehr anstrengend.
Examiner	Das tut mir leid. Wie alt ist denn ihre Großmutter?
Candidate	Sie ist 72 Jahre alt. Aber darum geht es nicht. Das Programm ist zu voll. Immer müssen wir etwas machen. Es gibt nicht genug Zeit zum Ausruhen. Meine Großmutter ist ganz erschöpft. Sie ist so müde, daß sie kaum noch etwas ansehen möchte.
Examiner	Aber Sie wußten doch, daß diese Reise eine Studienfahrt ist. Wir wollen unseren Gästen viel zeigen.
Candidate	Das stimmt. Aber jetzt möchte meine Großmutter sich ausruhen. Können wir viel- leicht drei Tage hier im Hotel bleiben? Am Freitag treffen wir die Gruppe dann in Genf wieder, so daß wir dann am Wochenende mit nach England zurückfahren.
Examiner	Also, das geht nicht so einfach. Wir haben hier im Hotel nur für eine Nacht gebucht.
Candidate	Können Sie denn nicht prüfen, ob das Zimmer noch für drei weitere Nächte frei ist?
Examiner	Das geht vielleicht. Aber Sie müßten dann für die Übernachtungen selbst bezahlen.
Candidate	Das sehe ich nicht ein. Wir haben für neun Tage bezahlt. Und wenn wir hier bleiben, brauchen wir die Zimmer in den anderen Hotels nicht. Also müßten die Kosten schon gedeckt sein.
Examiner	Nein, nein. Jedes Hotel hat andere Preise. Wir haben die Zimmer preiswerter bekommen, als Einzelreisende. Also, wenn Sie hier bleiben wollen, vorausgesetzt das Zimmer ist frei, dann müßten Sie bezahlen.
Candidate	Also, meine Großmutter will und kann auf keinen Fall weiter. Es geht ihr nicht gut. Sie möchte sich ausruhen, ein paar Tage Ruhe in diesem Hotel würde ihr gut tun.

Examiner	*Ja, wenn es ihr so schlecht geht, sollten wir vielleicht einen Rücktransport nach England organisieren. Sie sind doch versichert.*
Candidate	*Nein, wir haben keine Reiseversicherung abgeschlossen.*
Examiner	*Das war vielleicht ein Fehler. Sie müssen die Rückfahrt selbst bezahlen.*
Candidate	*Das ist aber ungerecht. Wenn Sie das Programm der Reise nicht so vollgepackt hätten, wäre meine Großmutter nicht krank geworden. Sie müssen den Touristen auch Zeit zum Ausruhen geben. Die Planung der Reise ist nicht gut. Vielleicht können Sie das Programm ändern und einen freien Nachmittag geben.*
Examiner	*Sie müssen aber bitte an die anderen Reisenden denken. Sie wollen die Reise so machen, wie im Programm. Die anderen wollen die Schweiz sehen, interessieren sich für Geschichte und Kultur.*
Candidate	*Das interessiert meine Großmutter auch sehr. Sie war früher Lehrerin für Kunst und Geschichte. Deshalb haben wir diese Tour gebucht. Nur wußten wir nicht, wie heiß und drückend das Wetter hier ist. Können Sie wirklich nichts für uns machen?*
Examiner	*Ja, Sie können morgen hier im Hotel bleiben und sich ausruhen. Am späten Nachmittag holen wir Sie dann vor der Weiterfahrt nach Luzern ab. Ich werde mit der Rezeption im Hotel sprechen, so daß Sie in Ihrem Zimmer bleiben können. Auch können Sie die Terrasse und den Park benutzen. Wahrscheinlich geht es dann Ihrer Großmutter wieder besser. Sie ist eigentlich recht gesund und fit.*
Candidate	*Das ist eine gute Idee. Ich glaube, das ist genau das Richtige. Vielen Dank für Ihre Mühe. Ich gehe jetzt zur Großmutter und erzähle ihr von Ihrem Vorschlag. Nochmals vielen Dank.*
Examiner	*Gern geschehen. Wir wollen, daß alle Reisenden einen guten Urlaub haben.*

PRACTICE PAPER 3 – READING AND WRITING (APPROX. ONE HOUR)

Question 1

Heroin am Schein

Die Postbank will künftig ihre allgemeinen Geschäftsbedingungen strenger handhaben, um Drogenhändlern die Geldwäsche zu erschweren. In einem internen Rundschreiben weist das Unternehmen jetzt seine Schalterangestellten an, bei dubiosen Bareinzahlungen die Annahme zu verweigern. Anlaß für die Aktion ist ein Brief des Hamburger Bürgermeisters Henning Voscherau. Der SPD-Politiker hatte sich bei Bundespostminister Bötsch (CSU) darüber beschwert, daß sich die Post als 'Geldwäscheanlage' mißbrauchen lasse. So war der Polizei ein junger Türke aufgefallen, der in einem Hamburger Postamt 10 000 Mark im Plastikbeutel auf den Tresen legte – an den Scheinen klebten noch Heroin-Reste, wie spätere Untersuchungen ergaben. Rund 200 Millionen Mark an Drogengewinnen sind nach Schätzung der Fahnder im vergangenen Jahr allein aus der Hansestadt über den Postweg in die Türkei transferiert worden. Bislang hatte die Postbank stets auf ihre Beförderungspflicht verwiesen, die ihr verbiete, Kunden vom Postverkehr auszuschließen. Die neue Regelung nutzt nun eine Vorschrift, die es der Bank erlaubt, Leistungen zu verweigern, wenn 'dies aus Gründen des öffentlichen Interesses notwendig ist.'

(*Der Spiegel* 32/1993)

(a) Finden Sie im Text Wörter, die den Folgenden entsprechen:

(i)   in Zukunft   (iv) überführt
(ii) zweifelhaft   (v)   bis jetzt
(iii) Ladentisch   (vi) wegen

(b) Beantworten Sie auf deutsch die folgenden Fragen, ohne dabei Wörter oder Sätze vom Text abzuschreiben:

   (i)   Was sollen Angestellte der Post in Zukunft nicht mehr machen?   [2]
   (ii) Warum war der junge Türke in Hamburg aufgefallen?   [2]
   (iii) Warum hatte die Post bis jetzt keine Kunden abgewiesen?   [2]
   (iv) Was schreibt die neue Regelung der Post vor?   [3]

Question 2

Zwei Tage in Trance

Wie Verbrechensopfer auf Einbruchdiebstähle reagieren

Susanne Kappel, 38, hat es immer wieder versucht. Abends, gegen halb elf, steht sie auf dem Hausflur. Wie früher zieht sie Straßenschuhe und Mantel an, geht zur Haustür und drückt auf die Klinke. Doch weiter kommt sie nicht. Seit dem 8. November des vorvergangen Jahres ist in Susanne Kappels Leben vieles anders geworden. Sie hat Angst, Herzklopfen, Bluthochdruck, traut sich nicht mehr im Dunkeln auf die Straße. Am 8. November war ein Einbrecher in ihre Wohnung eingedrungen.

'Ganz ruhig und besonnen' habe sie die Polizei informiert, anschließend den Notdienst der Bank angerufen, um die gestohlenen Schecks sperren zu lassen. 'Es war, als stünde ich neben mir', erzählt die selbstbewußte Frau, die nie zuvor derartige psychische Probleme kannte. Kurz darauf kam die Polizei, die Beamten nahmen den Einbruch auf und gingen wieder.

Erst dann, nach zwei Stunden, kam der Schock. Vor dem Waschbecken sackte Susanne Kappel zusammen. 'Fast zwei Tage' lebte sie in 'einer Art Trance'. Das Gefühl, 'die könnten wiederkommen', treibt sie bis heute, anderthalb Jahre nach der Tat, immer wieder ans Schlafzimmerfenster, wenn nachts ein leises Knacken zu hören ist. Den Weg vom Auto zur Haustür bringt sie abends nur hinter sich, wenn ihr Mann dabei ist: 'Ich hupe, er kommt raus, und wir gehen zusammen rein.'

Der Fall der Dieburgerin ist symptomatisch. 'Angst, Schlaflosigkeit, Depressionen, sogar Selbstmordgedanken' trieben viele Einbruchsopfer um, berichtet Günther Deegener von der Universitätsklinik Homburg. Der Psychologe hat die Schicksale mehrere hundert Opfer von Eigentumsdelikten untersucht.

'Viele der Betroffenen brechen ihre sozialen Kontakte weitgehend ab', berichtet Deegener. Sie versuchten 'sich abzuschotten, immer mit der Angst, es könnte wieder passieren'. Den Betroffenen werde durch das Eindringen in den 'Intimbereich Wohnung' eine Rückzugsmöglichkeit genommen. Die eigenen vier Wände entfielen als 'Oase zum Auftanken'.

(*Der Spiegel* 32/1993)

(a) Beantworten Sie auf deutsch die folgenden Fragen:

   (i)   Was hatte sich am 8. November bei Susanne Kappel ereignet?   [1]
   (ii) Wie hatte Susanne zuerst auf dieses Ereignis reagiert?   [1]
   (iii) Welche Folgen hat der Vorfall vom 8. November für Susanne?   [3]
   (iv) Wie erklärt der Psychologe Deegener das Verhalten von Einbruchsopfern? [3]

(b) Wie sollte man Opfern von Verbrechen helfen, damit sie über den Schrecken der Tat besser hinwegkommen? Beziehen Sie sich in Ihrer Antwort auf die beiden Texte. Schreiben Sie etwa 140 Wörter auf deutsch.   [15]

Question 3

CARING FOR THE AGED

At the present time in Germany there are around nine million people who are over 65 years of age, and this figure will continue to rise. The problems caused by this development are already beginning to emerge. They are worrying not only pension fund managers and medical insurance companies, but also increasingly middle-aged women. It is they who are expected to care for the old people involved. Almost exclusively it is considered the daughter's job to take on the extra responsibility of caring for sick or elderly parents.

Nursing a relative at home can affect one's career. In the case of women who began nursing a seriously ill relative at a comparatively early age 56% had experienced problems at work as a result. According to 28% of the women it had also had a detrimental effect on their financial position.

Another figure makes the seriousness of the situation even clearer. More than half those nursing a relative are themselves receiving medical treatment. The continual strain of providing adequate care and attention wears down the 'nurses' so much that they then eventually need to be 'nursed' themselves and become dependent on the help of others.

As a result of medical progress such care is now also needed for longer periods than in the past; this places even greater strains on the next generation of helpers. It is like an endless circle which can only continue as long as families are willing to play the good Samaritan – free of charge. Otherwise the costs would be so great that they would eventually lead to the collapse of the whole welfare system.

Gradually the Government is attempting to help those who provide such care, for example, by allowing the time involved to be taken into consideration when calculating pensions. It is also planned to provide support for a more flexible approach to working hours. Part-time work is being encouraged. Those who care for the elderly should also be able to interrupt their careers without being disadvantaged as a result and financial help is to be provided.

In housing policy there is a return to the old ideal of the extended family. In order to prevent the problems and illnesses caused by social isolation, 'multigeneration households' are being increasingly encouraged and financial help with the rent offered. Where this is not possible, different generations should be able to live in separate flats as neighbours who can provide mutual assistance.

A German acquaintance would like you to help her understand the points made in this article. Respond to the requests set out below.

Beantworten Sie bitte die folgenden Fragen auf deutsch:

(a) Warum beginnt man in Deutschland Probleme zu haben? [4]
(b) Warum geht das Frauen eher als Männer an? [4]
(c) Warum spricht man von einem 'endless circle'? [4]
(d) Warum wird der Streß größer für jede neue Generation? [4]

UCLES

ANSWERS TO PRACTICE PAPER 3

Question 1

(a) (i) künftig   (iv) transferiert
    (ii) dubios   (v) bislang
    (iii) Tresen   (vi) aus Gründen

(b) (i) Sie sollen keine fragwürdigen Geldeinzahlungen annehmen/zulassen. [1+1]
    (ii) Er hatte 10 000 Mark in einer Plastiktüte, die er einzahlen wollte. [1+1]
    (iii) Die Post muß alles transportieren, was ihr gebracht wird. [1+1]

(iv) Sie brauchen Leute nicht mehr zu bedienen, wenn so etwas für die Öffentlichkeit nicht gut wäre. [1+1+1]

Question 2

(a) (i) Man war in ihr Haus eingebrochen/Ein Dieb war in ihr Haus eingebrochen.
   (ii) Sie war ganz gefaßt/ruhig und hat die Polizei gerufen.
   (iii) Sie hat Angst davor, daß wieder ein Einbrecher kommt; sie hat Angst, nachts- auf die Straße zu gehen; sie kann nicht mehr alleine abends vom Auto ins Haus gehen; sie kann nicht mehr gut schlafen. (3 out of these 4)
   (iv) Die Opfer haben kein Vertrauen mehr in die Sicherheit ihres Hauses/Die Opfer glauben nicht, daß sie in ihrem Haus oder Wohnung sicher sind.

Examiner's note Question (iv) asks for a summary of the arguments given by Günther Deegener.

(b) This question takes the form of an essay. You are allowed to draw from the material in both texts and need to reformulate it in your words. Marks are awarded for content and for quality of language, which means grammatical accuracy, range of vocabulary and fluency. The better the material from the two texts is integrated into your own work, the higher this mark will be. Candidates who simply repeat information given without adapting the language and adding their own ideas will not score very highly.

Sample answer:

Es geht hier um ein großes Problem, das oft unterschätzt wird. Selbst Leute. die bei dem eigentlichen Delikt nicht anwesend waren, tragen oft schwer an den Folgen, wie es der Fall von Susanne Kappel zeigt. Es ist wichtig, daß man den entstandenen Sachschaden entschädigt (was meistens die Versicherung tut). Darüberhinaus müßte man auch eine psychologische Betreuung der Opfer garantieren. Vielleicht wäre es möglich, Selbsthilfegruppen, einzurichten, wo sich die Opfer von ähnlichen Delikten gegenseitig beraten könnten. Auf diese Weise würden auch did Kosten für eine Unterstützung nicht zu hoch werden.

Als zweiter Schritt sollte den Opfern gezeigt werden, wie sie in Zukunft ähnliche Situationen vermeiden können. Dazu gehören nicht nur Kurse in Selbstverteidigung, sondern auch Beratung in Sicherheitsfragen, damit man zum Beispiel weiteren Einbrüchen vorbeugen kann, und Training für Schalterbeamte und Verkaufspersonal, die Opfer von Betrügern wurden. So wie im ersten Text dargestellt, wurden Postbeamte Opfer von Drogenhändlern, indem sie unehrlich erworbenes Geld weiterleiteten.

Durch besseres Training werden die Beamten auf jene Menschen schneller aufmerksam und können so Schaden von der Post und weiten Teilen der Bevölkerung abwenden.

Question 3

(a) Die Anzahl von Leuten über 65 Jahre alt; der weitere Anstieg dieser Zahl.
(b) Von Frauen wird erwartet, daß sie die Versorgung der Alten übernehmen; man glaubt, dies sei eine Verpflichtung der Töchter.
(c) Die Frauen, die für ältere Verwandte sorgen, müssen selbst versorgt werden, weil sie davon krank werden.
(d) Weil die Generationen jetzt getrennt und isoliert wohnen; die Generationen sollten sich gegenseitig helfen, indem sie nicht weit voneinander wohnen.

Examiner's note You are asked to give the sense of the original without providing a word-for-word translation. As long as communication of the main points requested is achieved, paraphrase and circumlocution are acceptable. In the example paper there are four marks for each answer, two for elements of content and two for correctness of German. Each answer requires two statements drawn from the text.

PRACTICE PAPER 4 – WRITING
(APPROX. ONE AND A HALF HOURS)

Most examination boards set combined reading and writing papers and a separate essay paper. In some cases, there may even be a special letter-writing paper. The following is not a typical example of a question paper but rather a collection of typical questions, which would not normally be grouped together like this.

Question 1

In einer englischen Tageszeitung sehen Sie die folgende Annonce:

> **Au-pair gesucht für Arztfamilie in Winterthur, Schweiz. Zwei Kinder: 6 und 9 Jahre alt, zwei Hunde und zwei Pferde. Reitmöglichkeit.**
>
> **Führerschein erwünscht. Freie Kost und Logis sowie Taschengeld. Bewerbungen mit Bild an: Box No. 471 39.**

Da Sie vor dem Studium ein freies Jahr geplant haben, schreiben Sie eine Bewerbung. (200 Wörter)

Question 2

(advert reproduced courtesy of Wilhelm Heyne Verlag)

Haben Bücher in der heutigen Zeit noch eine Chance? Schreiben Sie etwa 250 Wörter.

Question 3

Advertisement of German Association VDV and German
National Railway DB AG. Reproduced with courtesy of Verband
Deutscher Verkehrsunternehmen

Wie sehen Sie die Zukunft für öffentliche Verkehrsmittel? Schreiben Sie etwa 250
Wörter.

Question 4

Katastrophenhilfe

Lahme Einsatztruppe

Bundeskanzler Helmut Kohl ist mit seinem Vorhaben, für internationale humanitäre Einsätze ein ziviles deutsches Hilfskorps zu bilden, offenbar am beharrlichen Widerstand der privaten und kirchlichen Hilfsorganisationen gescheitert.

1994 hatte Kohl angesichts der Flüchtlingskatastrophe im afrikanischen Bürgerkriegsland Ruanda die Idee von Drittwelt-Experten aufgegriffen, Katastrophen-Spezialisten in einer eigenständigen, jederzeit einsatzbereiten Helfer-Truppe zu organisieren. Das Hilfskorps, begeisterte sich der Kanzler seinerzeit, könne für junge Menschen auch eine Alternative zur Bundeswehr sein. Als der SPD-Parlamentarier Hans Wallow jetzt nachfragte, „welche

Schritte zur Umsetzung dieses Vorhabens" die Bonner Regierung inzwischen unternommen habe, wurde er beschieden, man wolle nun die Erfahrungen mit einem neuen „Koordinierungsmechanismus" zwischen Regierung und Hilfsorganisationen abwarten. Die Korps-Idee werde einstweilen nicht weiterverfolgt, so das Auswärtige Amt, um die „Vielfalt und Eigenständigkeit" der Hilfswerke zu wahren.

Source: Der Spiegel, March 1996. Reproduced with courtesy of SpiegelVerlag

Sollte es Aufgabe der europäischen Staaten sein, bei Katastrophen in Afrika und
Asien zu helfen?

POSSIBLE ANSWERS

Question 1

Sehr geehrte Familie,
ich habe Ihre Annonce in The Independent vom 12.06.1997 gelesen und möchte mich um die Stelle als Au-pair in Ihrem Haushalt bewerben.

Mein Name ist Barbara Rees, und ich bin 18 Jahre alt. In diesem Monat werde ich nach meinen Prüfungen mit der Schule fertig. Ich bin in der Oberstufe der Hyde County High School in Newtown, England. Ich habe Deutsch, Spanisch und Geschichte studiert. Vor Beginn meines Studiums an der Universität von Durham möchte ich ein Jahr im Ausland verbringen.

Ich habe zwei jüngere Brüder, auf die ich oft aufpasse, wenn meine Eltern ausgehen. Außerdem helfe ich meiner Mutter mit einer Spielgruppe für Kleinkinder, so daß ich einige Erfahrung im Umgang mit Kindern habe.

Was mich an Ihrer Anzeige besonders interessiert, ist die Möglichkeit zu reiten. Ich bin seit 6 Jahren Mitglied im örtlichen Reitverein und nehme regelmäßig an kleineren und mittleren Turnieren teil.

Leider habe ich noch keinen Führerschein, aber ich hoffe, im Juli meine Fahrprüfung zu bestehen.

Ich hoffe, bald von Ihnen zu hören,
mit freundlichen Grüßen

Question 2

Ich glaube, daß es immer einen Platz für Bücher geben wird. Natürlich darf man die Entwicklung von Computern und anderen Medien der Informationsverarbeitung nicht vergessen. Es wird heute immer mehr Material auf CD-ROM und Computerdisketten angeboten, das mit einem Computer abgerufen werden kann. Attraktive Beispiele dafür sind die 'Encarta' und ähnliche Nachschlagewerke auf CD.

Trotz dieser technischen Fortschritte in der Datenverarbeitung darf man nicht vergessen, daß man zu all diesen Dingen auch teure Geräte benötigt. Das ergibt doch einen wesentlichen Nachteil gegenüber Büchern. Man kann ohne technische Geräte lesen, jederzeit und an jedem Ort. Egal ob zu Hause, auf dem Weg zur Schule oder zum Büro, überall kann man sich die Zeit mit einem Buch vertreiben.

Gegenüber Film, Fernsehen und Video hat das Buch den Vorteil, daß man etwas immer wieder lesen kann, so oft und so schnell oder langsam wie man will. Jeder, der die Nachrichten im Radio oder Fernsehen verfolgt, hat es schon erlebt, daß man durch Unachtsamkeit etwas verpaßt. In einem Buch kann man eine Seite oder einen Satz so lange lesen, bis man ihn richtig verstanden hat.

Alles in allem bin ich der Meinung, daß Bücher nicht von anderen Medien verdrängt werden. Auch in fünfzig oder hundert Jahren wird man noch immer lesen.

Question 3

Zunehmende Zahlen von Autos, steigende Benzinpreise und immer größerer Mangel an Parkplätzen werden schon bald mehr Menschen dazu zwingen, öffentliche Verkehrsmittel zu benutzen. Unsere Städte ersticken in den Abgasen des Individualverkehrs. Deshalb ist es im Interesse von allen, so bald wie möglich auf Busse und Bahnen umzusteigen.

Die Bemühungen der Bundesbahn in Deutschland zeigen, wie ein Verkehrssystem der Zukunft aussehen kann. Attraktive Züge und pünktliche Busse helfen den Reisenden, ihr Ziel so schnell wie möglich zu erreichen. Saubere Bahnhöfe und geschützte Bushaltestellen tragen sicher mit dazu bei, daß mehr Autofahrer von der Straße auf die Schiene wechseln.

Jedoch sind geräumige und bequeme Züge nur ein Teil einer besseren Verkehrspolitik. Das Preissystem für Fahrten mit Bus und Bahn muß geändert werden. Es geht nicht, daß die Preise ständig steigen und zum Teil Einfachfahrkarten teurer als Rückfahrkarten sind. Nur mit einer günstigen Preisstruktur können langfristig neue Fahrgäste gewonnen werden.

Obwohl die Zukunft für öffentliche Verkehrsmittel gut aussieht, muß man noch viel tun, um das Angebot für die Reisenden noch reizvoller zu machen.

Question 4

Die im Spiegel-Artikel genannte Einsatzgruppe für humanitäre Hilfe ist eine ausgezeichnete Idee. Es sollte kein Zweifel darüber bestehen, daß alle Industrieländer den benachteiligten Staaten der Welt helfen sollten.

Durch die modernen Technologien der Nachrichtenvermittlung erfahren wir alle unmittelbar, was in anderen Teilen der Welt geschieht. Kein Krieg oder Umweltkatastrophe bleibt verborgen. Wir wissen morgen bestimmt, was heute irgendwo passiert ist. Dieses Wissen bedeutet Verantwortung. Keiner, weder Staaten noch Individuen, können sich damit herausreden, daß sie von dem Unglück anderer nichts gewußt haben.

Dazu kommt, daß der Reichtum Europas auch die Verpflichtung zur Hilfeleistung mit sich bringt. Schließlich war Europa nicht immer in dieser günstigen Position des Wohlstandes. Nach dem zweiten Weltkrieg halfen die USA in großzügiger Weise beim Wiederaufbau in Deutschland und anderen betroffenen Ländern. So ist es ohne Zweifel, daß Europa jetzt an der Reihe ist, anderen zu helfen. Keine Ausgabe sollte dafür als Unnütz angesehen werden. Wer weiß, vielleicht kommt es schon bald zur Wende, wenn man in Europa nur mit Hilfe der Unterstützung aus Übersee überleben kann.

LONGMAN
EXAM
PRACTICE
KITS

REVISION PLANNER

No. of weeks before the exams	Date: Week commencing	MONDAY	TUESDAY
12			
11			
10			

Getting Started — *Begin on week 12*

Use a calendar to put dates onto your planner and write in the dates of your exams. Fill in your targets for each day. Be realistic when setting the targets, and try your best to stick to them. If you miss a revision period, remember to re-schedule it for another time.

Get Familiar — *Weeks 12 and 11*

Identify the topics on your syllabuses. Get to know the format of the papers – time, number of questions, types of questions. Start reading through your class notes, coursework, etc.

Get Serious — *Week 10*

Complete reading through your notes – you should now have an overview of the whole syllabus. Choose 12 topics to study in greater depth for each subject. Allocate two topic areas for each subject for each of the next 6 weeks

Titles Available –

GCSE
Biology
Business Studies
Chemistry
English
French
Geography
German
Higher Maths
Information
Systems
Mathematics
Physics
Science

A-LEVEL
Biology
British and European
  Modern History
Business Studies
Chemistry
Economics
French
Geography
German
Mathematics
Physics
Psychology
Sociology

There are lots of ways to revise. It is important to find what works best for you. Here are some suggestions:

- try testing with a friend: testing each other can be fun!
- label or highlight sections of text and make a checklist of these items.
- learn to write summaries – these will be useful for revision later.
- try reading out loud to yourself.
- don't overdo it – the most effective continuous revision session is probably between forty and sixty minutes long.
- practise answering past exam papers and test yourself using the same amount of time as you will have on the actual day – this will help to make the exam itself less daunting.
- pace yourself, taking it step by step.

WEDNESDAY	THURSDAY	FRIDAY	SATURDAY	SUNDAY

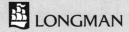